CHRISTIANS IN THE FIRING LINE

CHRISTIANS IN THE FIRING LINE

DR RICHARD SCOTT

WILBERFORCE
PUBLICATIONS

London

First published in Great Britain in 2013 by
Wilberforce Publications
70 Wimpole Street, London W1G 8AX
All rights reserved.

ISBN 978-0-9575725-1-5

Printed in Great Britain by Imprint Digital, Exeter
and
Printed worldwide by Createspace

Contents

*The book is dedicated to
Andrea and Paul and all at Christian Concern.
Without your help, we would all be in a worse position.*

Thanks

*Firstly, to my wife, Heather, and my GP colleagues
who supported me and covered for me while I was
undergoing surgery, chemo and radiotherapy.
The time off also enabled me to write this book.*

*Secondly, to Libby at Christian Concern for
locating and cheerfully sending me legal reports.*

*Lastly to our GP secretaries, Chris and Tracy, who,
despite work pressures, indefatigably and competently
made up for my IT deficiencies time and again!
Without your help, I would be in a worse position.*

Foreword

This is a courageous book by a courageous man who is himself one of the cases discussed here. We don't have to agree with every word of the author's or of those mentioned here to admire them not only for their courage but also for their persistence and their faithfulness sometimes in the face of overwhelming odds.

The thirteen cases mentioned here represent many more that have either come to court or been settled in some other way. They included both those that have been won and those that have been lost, as well as those that have not yet been settled. Richard Scott is meticulously fair in describing how a particular case has arisen and how it has been dealt with, its weaknesses and strengths – even his own!

We are made aware immediately of the price to be paid and the cost involved whether it is loss of employment, the threat of being struck off the registers of professional bodies or just unpopularity in the community or the media.

We are left with a pervasive sense of fear in officialdom brought about by aggressive secularism, as well as radical LGBT and Islamist lobbies. This results in excruciating political correctness to placate these vociferous lobbies and Christians are often the main sufferers. We have the now familiar scenario of special interest lobbies dominating public life and public discourse with dire consequences for anyone who challenges them. At the same time, they know how to play the victim and elicit public sympathy for themselves.

Apart from questions of truth raised by these cases, we have some systemic issues raised by them. In my experience, the exclusion from employment or participation in public life, which the people in these cases have tasted, as well as discrimination because of belief, which they have also experienced, is often the beginning of persecution. Britain has had a long moral and legal tradition of respecting conscience, even in times of war but also in the context of controversial legislation such as the Abortion Act of 1967.

In more recent legislation, however, especially on 'equality', there seems not to be any protection for people's consciences, even those formed by well-known spiritual and moral traditions, such as the Christian. Nor have we learnt any lessons from across the Atlantic about how to accommodate people's beliefs at the work place or in public service. It has been noted, time and time again, that if no provision is made for conscience and reasonable accommodation, we will soon be in a totalitarian situation in the name of 'liberal' values.

As Dr Scott points out, the marginalisation and discrimination experienced by Christians here does not amount to the virulent persecution they experience elsewhere. They are not generally at risk of life or limb, though they can be threatened, arrested or lose their livelihood. The Church here, nevertheless, needs now, and urgently, to learn from their brothers and sisters overseas about how to bear Christian witness in difficult situations.

Christian Concern and the Christian Legal Centre are right in the spotlight as they seek to represent Christians under pressure. It is only the high-profile cases that get publicity but a great deal of back-room work goes on all the time to secure justice for people unfairly dealt with. Sometimes this is through painstaking negotiation or mediation. At other times, there is action in the courts or tribunals. They are not afraid of losing and, above all, they give hope to those who come up against the relentless hostility of the lobbies and the compliant political correctness of public bodies and officials. It must be most encouraging to know that there is someone to turn to in an hour of need.

Richard Scott has done us a great service by bringing these cases to the attention of the wider public. I hope the merits of them will be fairly considered in the days and months to come.

Bishop Michael Nazir-Ali
21 June 2013

Preface

My wife and I were preparing to work overseas as medical
missionaries and were studying together at one of the Selly
Oak Colleges (in Birmingham), where we loved mixing
with our fellow students who came from many different
countries. That was over twenty years ago, but we still recall
two particularly memorable lecturers. One was an Indian
who took a shine to us (maybe because we had previously
worked amongst Hindus in his country). It was from him
that we learnt to appreciate a proper Balti! The other taught
with great passion on Islam. A linguist who spoke twenty
languages, his grasp of Arabic and love for his subject would
have led some to think he was an authentic Muslim – had his
job title not revealed his true calling as a Christian minister.
What we learnt from him prepared us well for our subsequent
work in rural north-eastern Tanzania. Muslims predominated
in that region, but they and their Christian neighbours got
on very well together – they were determined to do so.
Intermarriage was common, and successive children in the
same family were often brought up in the different faiths
alternately – one attending the mosque, the next going to
church – although admittedly such a compromise raised
many questions in my mind.

Having enjoyed such good inter-faith relations, we were nevertheless aware that the situation around the world was somewhat less idyllic. Returning to the UK in the mid-1990s, we began to support the work of Barnabas Fund and CSW, two organisations that act as advocates for Christians persecuted for their faith abroad. The stories are shocking: Nigerian Christians are frequently butchered, whilst the number of those in Iraq has been greatly reduced as many flee to safety abroad. In Egypt, Christians struggle to make a living at the bottom of the labour market, victimised as they take the blame for their country's ills. In India, many have suffered appallingly at the hands of Hindu extremists.

All seems pretty desperate, but dreadful though their situations are, the temptation for us, their brothers and sisters in Christ, is simply to pray and send money before moving on in our busy lives. In so doing, we may not only be doing them a disservice but missing the bigger picture.

For most Christians living in the UK, life is relatively easy. Appalling tales from far away, in cultures remote from our own, stir our consciences briefly, but it can be hard to identify truly with those who are suffering – after all, we have probably never been in a comparable position, nor been faced with agonising life and death decisions like those they have to deal with. Instead, we are grateful and hold on to the idea that the UK remains a "Christian country", a place where we are safe to express our faith in peace. Complacency can set in, along with the attitude that, "we do things differently here". That can obscure what is beginning to happen in our country today.

You don't have to be a Christian to be aware that Muslim converts to Christianity remain in grave danger, even in the UK. Newspapers report instances of converts having to leave their families to avoid severe reprisal. The danger is that we see this as a problem affecting others – in this case a tiny section of society, brave people whose misfortune is perceived as being as much cultural as religious. We may even applaud them for suffering so much for their faith – our faith. Wondering whether, but for an accident of birth, we would have the guts to do likewise, appears academic, even fanciful, for the need and opportunity to make a costly stand for our faith seems hardly likely to arise. Or will it?

Christianity in this country is under threat as never before. Last year, national newspapers reported a High Court judgment banning prayer in council meetings. The case had been brought by an atheist councillor, backed up by the National Secular Society, whose intention is to go further. Their targets include the formal prayers in both Houses of Parliament and the daily acts of worship in community schools. Moreover, this spring, Parliament is debating an amendment to allow for gay marriage, while Lord Falconer is once again attempting to legalise assisted suicide. Both of these measures, while having a veneer of empathy and respectability, go directly against God's stated Word, and yet to speak out against them has led to some UK Christians being ostracised for their views. But some are prepared to do so, and Lord Carey, the former Archbishop of Canterbury, has hit back, horrified that the Christian voice in this country is being silenced by creeping secularisation. The danger is that secularism becomes the new orthodoxy, with Christianity increasingly marginalised.

While the high priest of new atheism, Richard Dawkins, considers anyone believing in God to be brainless and dangerous to the health of the nation, we beg to disagree, looking to our bishops, church leaders and even the Queen to fight on our behalf, putting the case for faith. It is easy for individual Christians to adopt the role of chattering spectator, allowing our religious bosses to tackle the big issues confronting us today – atheism, secularism, humanism and political correctness. For most of us do not really see such battles as *our* problem, *our* fight. As yet, the secular agenda has not impacted us too badly as individuals, so we try not to worry, we don't get involved, and we leave it to others to sort out. And if they don't, and if those without religious conviction make further inroads into the religious life and practice of this country, well, isn't that simply in line with biblical teaching that things will get worse for believers until Jesus returns? Then all will be well... Until then, let's keep our heads down and get on with it.

This book documents the stories of those who have chosen to think and act differently, and an organisation dedicated to acting likewise.

About Christian Concern

Christian Concern dates only from 2008, but the idea behind the organisation was first mooted in 2003. Barrister Andrea Minichiello Williams and human rights barrister Paul Diamond had both been members of the Lawyers' Christian Fellowship (LCF). Difficult cases involving Christian freedoms were coming up which they took on – with three instances particularly memorable.

Harry Hammond was an elderly preacher who was beaten up by gay activists in Bournemouth in 2004. Of one mind with Andrea, Paul Diamond agreed to represent him and appealed on his behalf, outraged that in this country such violent behaviour was rewarded by the police arresting the victim instead of the protagonists. The incident acted as a catalyst in confirming their desire to act on behalf of Christians in trouble for their faith. Subsequently, in 2006, Nadia Eweida was dismissed by BA for wearing a cross at work, and then, in 2007, Exeter University ruled that their Christian Union could not stipulate that membership was for Christians only.

Outrageous? Extraordinary? One might think so, but as the number of cases rapidly escalated, developments in

Parliament gave further grounds for concern.The Religious Hatred Bill (2006) threatened to prevent Christians from proclaiming the primacy of Jesus Christ, with serious potential consequences for freedom of evangelism. In the light of these problems, it became clear that counter-attack through a new body was needed. With several others also realising the need to respond urgently, Christian Concern came into being. Started in a small, almost ramshackle fashion, the organisation has been blessed, growing rapidly over the last half-decade. Benefitting from the donation of wonderful premises, staff numbers are increasing, enabling more activity. Supporters now number 60,000.

Christian Concern and its sister organisation the Christian Legal Centre now work together to speak of Jesus Christ in public life. The CLC deals with individual legal cases, including taking them as far as the European Court of Human Rights in Strasbourg, whilst Christian Concern campaigns against unjust laws and policies, providing a strong Christian voice on a broad range of topics. This leads to coverage in the media, with many opportunities to share the gospel in this country and internationally.

At this time, churches and individual Christians more than ever need to be enabled to engage with contemporary issues. To this end, Christian Concern provides up to date information, resources and tools to help people respond to and pray about the current political assaults on Christian freedoms. With a particular desire to see a new generation of Christian leaders in this country, Christian Concern has set up the Wilberforce Academy which prepares young professionals for public life.

Through all this work, those in need will contact Christian Concern or the CLC for help. Some will approach the organisation early, looking for advice, whilst others will get in touch towards the end of the line, with their situations seemingly hopeless. Either way, these Christian lawyers will respond and react on their behalf – as they did in my case.

Richard Scott

Introduction

Well before I needed their services, I first encountered the work of the Christian Legal Centre (CLC) in October 2009. My wife and I attended a conference run by the Christian Medical Fellowship, entitled *Coming out as a Christian: Handling Conflict in the NHS*. In the course of the day, four doctors and nurses stood at the front while their cases were presented. Each had run into trouble with their professional organisations and other authorities through practising their Christian faith at work. Alongside them was Andrea Minichiello Williams, a lawyer, and Director of the CLC. She had represented the four and was thus very familiar with the legal position in each case, but what stood out was her passion and zeal for procuring justice for these humble medics who had really suffered for making a stand.

Very impressed by her, I was equally taken by the conference strapline: "It could be you next." As a GP-evangelist, I had already had a handful of minor complaints about outreach at work and was well aware that my working environment, the NHS, is not exactly avidly pro-Christian. But prior to the conference I had not properly appreciated the extent to which Christians, represented here by health professionals, could be under fire from authorities seemingly determined to get them. By the close of the event I was rather better informed. Deciding to introduce myself to Andrea, I mentioned that I, too, might need her help one day. Gracefully, she thought it unlikely – but I knew where to turn when that day did come.

God had given me advance notice of an organisation dedicated to supporting and acting as advocates for Christians in the UK. Others would discover the CLC in their hour of need. With the climate as it is, hundreds of people contact the CLC every year for help. Many are in grave need as their jobs are on the line. This book details thirteen of these cases, in which ordinary people have found themselves in exceptional circumstances. What were the issues that led them to contend for their faith? How did they respond and what was the result? Above all, did they remain men and women of faith or did their belief (and hope) diminish or disappear in the face of adversity?

Remember, it could be you next.

PART ONE

THE CROSS PROVES UNACCEPTABLE AT WORK

1

Shirley Chaplin
The Nurse

Shirley grew up in a small Somerset village as a quiet child who loved reading but was hopeless at sport! Taught right from the beginning to treat everyone as she would wish to be treated, she regularly attended Sunday School and was confirmed at the age of sixteen. Some might consider this rather delayed, but as someone who rarely did anything spontaneously it simply reflected her personality, as she preferred to think things through. During her confirmation she wore a silver cross and chain, a habit that has continued to the present day.

Some years later, she trained to be a nurse. She took some time off when her first child was born but then returned to work part-time after having her second child. Taking her job seriously she studied hard, undertaking a number of courses designed to benefit patient care, and in 2002 became deputy ward manager. Teaching others was now part of her remit and she gained immense job satisfaction from watching them develop. She also continued her own learning, studying for a BSc in Nursing Studies. Achieving this award in 2006 was very rewarding as she had not imagined when she began her career that she had the intellectual ability to obtain a degree. By this time she had been nursing for nearly thirty years, but alongside her professional development one thing stood out: Shirley was a Christian, and demonstrated this by wearing her cross throughout her time in the various nursing specialities in which she had been employed.

The Case

In June 2009, whilst working at the Royal Devon and Exeter NHS Trust Hospital, Shirley was approached by a Senior Matron and was asked for the very first time in her career to remove the cross and chain. Shirley declined as she regarded it not merely as an adornment but as a statement of her Christian faith. She was subsequently approached by a second Senior Matron but again declined to remove it. At this point matters escalated and she received a written letter informing her that she was in breach of the Trust's uniform policy, and she was invited to a meeting to discuss the issue further.

At the meeting, Shirley explained that the cross was very significant in terms of her faith and that she had worn it throughout her long nursing career without causing any problem with a patient or colleague until now. She added that being told to remove this sign of her faith had caused her extreme distress and that she wished to continue wearing it.

In reply, one of the Senior Matrons suggested that the cross be removed from her neck but carried in her pocket or pinned out of sight beneath her uniform. Shirley viewed this suggestion as disrespectful to her faith, having always worn her cross visibly since her confirmation back in 1971. Trying to find a way forward, she in turn proposed that she be allowed to wear a tee-shirt resembling the previous hospital uniform, as this had a collar which would place the chain out of sight from behind. But as tee-shirts did not comply with hospital uniform policy, this proved impossible to implement. The matter was deferred for a month.

In the interim, Shirley obtained the hospital uniform policy from 2007. It stated that, *any member of staff who wishes to wear particular types of clothes or jewellery for religious or cultural reasons must raise this with their line manager who will not unreasonably withhold approval*. As a result, Shirley concluded her seniors were not complying with this policy and that therefore she was being discriminated against.

Shirley was invited to a formal meeting on 20th July 2009. Whilst waiting for the meeting to begin, she glanced through a copy of the Trust News (dated May 2009), which clearly depicted nurses wearing necklaces on the front cover. During the meeting, she questioned why she was the only one facing disciplinary action for wearing a cross and chain when others were clearly also in breach of this same uniform policy, but was informed that all others were equally being told to remove any jewellery.

She then went on to highlight the exact wording in the uniform policy. Now she learnt that the Trust was saying that her necklace posed a health and safety risk. This was a new tactic employed by them, yet she had already investigated this possibility with the Health and Safety Executive who held no record of either a nurse or patient being harmed through a nurse wearing a necklace. Furthermore, her chain was of such fine gauge that she felt it would snap if ever pulled by a patient. When faced with these answers, the Senior Matron agreed that the risk of harm was small but remained adamant that the necklace should be removed. Redeployment was discussed and Shirley learnt that if she continued to be in breach of hospital policy she would be taken down a formal disciplinary route, a statement which was rapidly backed up by a formal letter to this effect.

Shirley had already mentioned to the Trust that removing

her cross at work would cause her considerable distress. As a result of the stand made by her employers she became so distressed that she began to sleep and function poorly, and had to be signed off work for two weeks by her GP because of stress. Coming back, she should have undergone a "return to work" interview by the ward matron but instead was interviewed in the office of a Senior Matron. The content of what took place had nothing to do with returning to work. Instead, a further discussion regarding her non-compliance with the uniform policy took place and Shirley was advised that continued disobedience in relation to management instruction would lead to a formal disciplinary process that would end in her dismissal.

Not having predicted this turn of events, Shirley became emotionally very distraught as she saw her hopes for a speedy return to work dashed. Occupational Health confirmed that she was suffering from emotional stress and advised that she should seek to resolve the issue of wearing her cross at work! Returning to work three days later, Shirley was assured that a meeting would take place between herself and the Senior Matron. But again, a "return to work" interview did not take place. Instead, a pensions expert had been summoned to provide advice on the financial implications of redeployment. For a decision concerning her working practice had been made: she could continue working on the ward, but now only in a non-clinical role. This was seen as preferable to the alternative – being suspended on full pay – for such a "valued team member". With the cards stacked against her, Shirley's church minister stepped in and rang the Christian Legal Centre. His input led to barrister Paul Diamond rapidly getting involved. By now in her early mid-fifties, at stake was not only her job but her pension. For the terms of any redeployment to be fair, her work grade and pay needed to remain the same, but her line manager had already made clear that these would not be guaranteed and thus her pension could fall. Equally, Paul knew that even if the redeployment offer was unsatisfactory, the Trust would still insist on her removing the cross, and that if she refused, a charge of insubordination could be lodged with dismissal resulting. Right from the beginning, the stakes were high.

A further meeting was planned for early September 2009. But it was postponed after Shirley requested clarification on two points. Firstly, was she allowed to pin her cross onto her uniform, as this would prevent the theoretical risk of injury to either her or a patient if the latter grabbed her chain? Secondly, why were other faiths permitted to wear religious apparel when the policy was being so vigorously enforced with her?

A third point also became obvious prior to the meeting. Previously, Shirley had pointed out that other staff members were clearly being permitted to wear jewellery, only to be informed again that they too were being told to remove the offending articles. So why was it that she encountered nurses, a therapist, pharmacists and housekeeping staff all with necklaces and wrist watches on show? Nurses, in particular, wore chains, and some with crosses attached. When questioned by Shirley, these staff members commented that no-one had ever asked them to remove personal items of jewellery. Finally, she noted that the wearing of a Medi-alert necklace – a heavy gauge chain – is permitted as it is not deemed a health and safety risk.

In acknowledging Shirley's points, the Trust responded that she could not pin her cross to her uniform. Equally, that members of other faiths were wearing religious apparel was not disputed as this was allowed by Trust policy. However, crucially this permission did not apply to her, as wearing a cross is not a mandatory requirement of the Christian faith!

The formal meeting duly took place on 10th September

2009, with her pastor and a work colleague supporting Shirley. When her turn came to speak, she asked why she was being singled out when others were manifestly failing to comply with the jewellery policy. Reassured that the policy was being equally applied and enforced throughout the hospital, the Trust squashed her argument and then again offered her redeployment in a non-clinical role. Effectively, Shirley was now being asked to choose between her faith and her nursing vocation.

Not wanting to lose her employment, Shirley suggested another way forward, based on what she had seen worn by her pastor's wife. It involved a chain fastened by two small magnets which parted if tugged, thus getting round any safety issues. The hospital countered by recommending she wear a tee shirt in corporate colours with the cross and chain held in place underneath.

Shirley considered the tee shirt option to be simply not acceptable. Not only disrespectful to her personally, it effectively required her to hide the public expression of her faith, something which the Trust did not apply to those of other faiths. Sadly, her innovative idea concerning the chain with the magnetic catch was also turned down, as the Trust felt that the cross itself might scratch and therefore harm somebody. The failure to agree to this middle ground was a great pity as Shirley had been prepared to compromise in order to continue within a profession she loved.

Redeployment in a non-clinical capacity allowed Shirley some contact with staff members but denied her direct patient contact. Viewing this as a form of dismissal, it was equally distressing to note that whilst the Trust claimed to be seeking a solution to enable her to return to clinical duties, they continued to ignore other members of staff working within the clinical environment whilst openly in breach of the uniform policy. In seeing the Trust utterly fail to apply their rules to others whilst doggedly pursuing them in her case, Shirley could only conclude that she was being openly victimised for displaying her commitment to the Christian faith through wearing her cross.

On 29th October 2009, Shirley lodged a claim with the Employment Tribunal for religious discrimination, on the advice of her legal counsel. She later received a letter from her Senior Matron with an alternative suggestion – namely that she consider wearing earrings, either studded or clip-on, in the shape of a cross. Shirley viewed this suggestion as an inadequate substitute for the cross and chain she had worn for all these years. And clip-on earrings would not only be easily dislodged and thus prove a far greater health and safety hazard, but again would not comply with the uniform policy!

By the end of November, Shirley was coping poorly with her redeployment. Stressed and tearful, she missed the support of long-established colleagues, and her sense of discrimination was heightened by hospital visitors reporting that other uniformed staff were continuing to wear items of personal jewellery. Worse still, her current role came with no structure or guaranteed long-term future. With no specific training attached, she felt that any failure on her part to carry out this role adequately would allow the Trust to dismiss her on grounds of capability.

Since then, with her tribunal claim unsuccessful, Shirley has taken the difficult decision to retire, rather than continue working for people who have no insight into how they have treated her. She believed that, even if she had been allowed back into clinical work, management would simply have waited for another opportunity to make her life as difficult as possible; having been treated once with utter contempt, she was not willing to face this prospect again.

During her working career, the Trust had set up (and Shirley had attended) various study days, during which respecting religious and cultural diversity was held up as the gold standard. In practice, however, the treatment she had received was inconsistent with this policy. For one thing, however, she is thankful. Only when challenged to choose between her love for nursing and her love for God did she realise – for the first time – just how strong her belief was.

This could have been the end of the matter. Shirley has never courted publicity and was initially very reluctant for the media to become involved. But the principle at stake was so important that she agreed to her case being taken further. Accordingly, an application was made by the Christian Legal Centre to the European Court of Human Rights (ECHR) at Strasbourg. Held in September 2012, with a judgment made in January 2013, her case has serious ramifications for the freedom of Christians in the UK and across Europe.

In the build-up to Strasbourg, the response of government ministers was fascinating....

A Downing Street spokesman revealed, "The Prime Minister's personal view is that people should be able to wear crosses." (12th March 2012)

The same day, when asked to respond to a Parliamentary Question whether, as part of his duties as Secretary of State, he will defend the rights of Christian local authority workers discreetly to wear crosses (or crucifixes) at work, as he would do of the rights of Sikhs to wear the turban, Eric Pickles MP responded, "It is certainly my view that, provided any object does not get in the way of someone doing their job, a discreet display of their religion is something that we should welcome."

What about a legal view? The Attorney General, Dominic Grieve, stated, "Employers need to have a specific and legitimate reason in order to restrict their employees from openly wearing a cross or any other religious item." (21st May 2012)

Finally, Lynne Featherstone, Minister for Equalities and Criminal Information, unequivocally stated that, "The grounds (for an employer to say "no" to wearing a cross) have to be reasonable and cannot be used as a backdoor way to discriminate against any religion. In addition, where a policy indirectly discriminates against those of a particular religion and this policy cannot be justified, that is also unlawful." (12th April 2012)

That would seem to be pretty clear. The government supports those wishing to wear a cross. Not so fast! For when the application to the ECHR was made, the government changed its tune. Submitting that the applicant's wearing of a visible cross was not a manifestation of her religion or belief within the meaning of Article 9, any restriction on this ability to wear a cross did not interfere with her rights as protected by Article 9. Incredibly, they went further, postulating that wearing a cross is not even a generally recognised form of practising the Christian faith as it was not a requirement of the faith to do so. Furthermore, should an individual wish to do so, they are, of course, free to resign and seek employment elsewhere! Such a "freedom" would guarantee their Article 9 rights in domestic law.

An extraordinary state of affairs, and one which clearly demonstrates the mismatch between governmental words and actions in this affair. In the midst of this governmental muddle, it is hard to see how in any way their submission was consistent with freedom of thought, conscience and religion. The worry was that, should they prove successful, the protections provided by Article 9 would effectively be privatised – i.e. have no bearing on involvement in mainstream public life.

Mr Diamond, in requesting referral to the ECHR, noted also that in 2010 the Department of Health modified health and safety requirements to accommodate minority faiths.

The new policy permits Sikhs and Muslims to avoid the "bare beneath the elbow" rule by the use of over-sleeves (paid for by public money and having an increased risk of infection) and the wearing of the kara bracelet. This new policy was based on the advice of Islamic scholars and the Muslim Spiritual Care Provision in the National Health Service. Essentially, the threshold of risk was lowered to accommodate religious practices.

He went on to state that there is no evidence of any injury caused by the cross in the entire history of the NHS and thus the risk is purely theoretical – and that her employer absurdly set itself up as a religious authority with the capacity to determine which religions to privilege and which faiths to disadvantage. The disadvantaging of the cross here, with evidence that other faiths were privileged, was a decision in line with Governmental pressure to pursue diversity policies, using the pretext of health and safety in this case. There was a duty on the employer to adjust, adapt or modify the workplace to reasonably accommodate religious rights. Finally, the court should remember that Mrs Chaplin had worked as a nurse since 1981, wearing her cross without incident, and that the risk inherent in wearing a hijab or kara bracelet means that the standard is "reasonable" not "absolute" safety.

Mr Diamond's final points concerned the marginalisation of Christians in the UK in more general terms. Aware that overall the UK has a good record on human rights, he cited a number of decisions made in recent years against Christians, which have attracted media attention and led to ridicule of the judiciary. For example, The Equality and Human Rights Commission (EHRC) submitted to a British court that the State should protect vulnerable children from being "infected" with Judaeo-Christian values on sexual morality, in arguing that a Christian family was unsuitable to foster children because they did not endorse homosexuality. Christian Unions have been suspended from universities for membership requirements including being a Christian prior to joining. Christian girls have been prevented from wearing chastity rings, preachers arrested for preaching "offensive" sermons from the Bible, and Christian guest house owners successfully sued for seeking to uphold a Christian ethos within their business. Catholic adoption agencies have been closed by the government, and Christian charities had their funding removed because of the nature of the charity. Access to venues is also being denied to Christian groups. On a wider European level, he also noted that the European Parliament has officially recognised the phenomenon of intolerance and discrimination against Christians, and held numerous workshops in order to stem the tide of aggressive secularism. He therefore submitted that the Convention rights of Mrs Chaplin had been violated by the UK.

Judgment took place in January 2013. Of the four applicants presented to the ECHR, two were represented by Christian Concern. In only one case – that of Nadia Eweida, a British Airways worker who had also been prevented from wearing a cross, did the court rule that the UK had violated Article 9. In the other three cases, the court ruled that the decisions of the domestic courts were within the wide "margin of appreciation (discretion)" accorded to States. Nevertheless, in each case, judgment was made that there had been interference with the individuals' Article 9 freedom.

Although Shirley's case was lost, the Christian Legal Centre took a very positive view on these rulings. This was the first time that the Court has ever found the UK in violation of Article 9. This is therefore highly significant for the understanding and practical application of freedom of thought, conscience and religion across the Council of Europe area. It represents a challenge to the UK's recent approach, and should prompt a further review of how the UK government and courts (and those of other member States) approach these matters in the future.

But the judgment did not give sufficient weight to Article 9 protections, not least the obligation to practise reasonable accommodation, leading to an unjustified restriction of freedom.

Noting that the judgment was not final, the CLC asked for Shirley's case to be referred to the Grand Chamber of the ECHR, but permission was denied at the end of May 2013. Nevertheless, Andrea Williams is convinced that none of this has been in vain. Much has been achieved along the way which will help in contending for Christian freedoms in UK courts in the future.

2

Colin Atkinson
The Van Driver

Colin was born in Wakefield in 1947 during one of the worst winters on record. His parents were both office caretakers and money was tight for the large and growing family. Colin arrived as the fifth child, and his childhood memories were sweet. Walking to Sunday School in the Zion Chapel was particularly memorable. In 1955 the family moved to York after his father got a job on the railways. For the children, this ushered in great adventure. Alongside other railway families, they could now spend their annual week's holiday travelling around the UK in obsolete rail carriages termed "camping coaches", hired at reduced rates.

Secondary school, though, came as a real shock for Colin; there were many scrapes as older boys threw newcomers over a wall in the playground, and made teachers' lives a misery. Glad to leave in 1962, tragedy struck just two weeks later when his beloved Dad collapsed and died on the way to work, aged just forty-seven. In shock, the family pulled together. Colin got a job loading mine cars going underground with supplies, and whilst there he was encouraged by the training officer to study at night. The next year he was accepted for an electrical apprenticeship.

Life wasn't all work, though. In the midst of the "swinging sixties" he enjoyed dancing with his girlfriend, whilst still helping his mother with her cleaning jobs. Becoming a fully fledged electrician in 1967, he married Jacqueline, his first wife, in 1969, and was blessed with three daughters, who are now his closest friends. Fed up with pit strikes, he joined the army in 1971 and was posted to Germany. Life was good, with daughter Alison being born one week after arrival, but Northern Ireland would prove very different.

With Sunday School days long gone, Colin had never actively sought God until now. The hatred and violence he encountered led him to the garrison chapel, and to accept prayer from the padre each Sunday. Reassured and peaceful, he knew that God was speaking to him. Equally, he remembered that God had protected his life during a motorbike phase in the 1960s when he had survived a series of crashes, including one sufficiently serious to badly damage his knee and foot and give him deep friction burns covering nearly two-thirds of his body. Other biking friends had not been so fortunate, with eight lads losing their lives in Wakefield the following year. In this context, he was now very aware of his disobedience in turning his back on a God he had at one time thought he did not need.

In 1977, Colin's life took another twist, with injury again playing its part. Having just completed an advanced electronics course, and with promotion to sergeant just a year away, he ruptured his knee ligaments playing football. Repair was not possible at that time and Colin was discharged from the army on medical grounds.

By now, in 1987, Colin and his wife were able to enjoy family life again and took their youngest daughter, Sally, to Brownies. God stepped in once more as the vicar, John Marsh, spoke about Jesus' encounter with Nicodemus. Colin knew that John was speaking directly to him, and felt both uncomfortable and overwhelmed. Challenged to respond that day, he didn't do so, but met with John two weeks later in order to understand what was happening.

Told that it was the work of the Holy Spirit and that his life would never be the same again, this proved to be the case. Jacqueline did not share his faith and, although she came to church occasionally, pressure was put on their family life. Friction developed, especially when he was involved with prison ministry and, the girls already having left home, in 2001 Jacqueline announced that she was divorcing him. Their marriage of thirty-one years was over.

In 2003, Colin moved into sheltered housing. As a result, he came into contact with a Christian lady, Geraldine, with whom he had much in common. They married in November 2004, went to Israel, and generally enjoyed serving God together. By now Colin had worked for some years for Wakefield District Housing (WDH) as an electrician. Aware that his new wife's fibromyalgia required him to spend more time with her, in late 2008 he asked his employer for a reduced working week. It took WDH eighteen months to finally sanction this application, even though it was part of company policy. This caused the Atkinsons a lot of stress, and when Colin finally wrote to the CEO, he was aware that some senior managers were unhappy about what had taken place. This particular disagreement pre-dated a rather bigger issue at work, which would soon cast a shadow over Colin's life.

The Case

As a working Christian, Colin had always discreetly displayed a palm cross on the dashboard of his company van. This had never proved problematic until the company received an anonymous complaint from a tenant using WDH's services towards the end of 2009. The complaint did not specifically target the presence of the cross in Colin's van, but instead was more generally applied to the use of the vehicle. Nevertheless, it included the following:

"... if passengers are ever carried in it, I can only hope they are of the Christian faith, the vehicle has a cross displayed in front of the driver, does this mean only Christians are allowed in or does WDH not care about offending other faiths?"

For the first time in seventeen years, Colin's cross had become an issue. His manager informed him that by displaying it he was breaking company rules and that the offending item must be removed from his dashboard. Colin refused to comply, despite the company placing him under huge pressure to adhere to their instruction by repeating their demands many times over the next five weeks. Threatened with dismissal, he urgently needed advice, and contacted the Christian Legal Centre in May 2010, whilst filing a grievance with his shop steward.

The grievance was based on Colin perceiving these orders to remove the cross as constituting harassment at work. He also challenged the company to demonstrate exactly which of their rules he was breaking, as he had become very concerned about the way WDH applied its own policies. The company couldn't, but did not back down. Later, they would amend company policy, inventing a rule that he would then be breaking by displaying his cross. But at this point in time the rule was absent. Nevertheless, the company's insistence on pursuing Colin over this issue led inevitably to much stress for both him and Geraldine.

As he reflected on the company's actions, it was clear that WDH were concerned that the cross in his van might cause the public to view the company as favouring Christianity, thus potentially causing offence and belying its status as a neutral organisation. What to him was a personal symbol of faith, to WDH was akin to a political statement. But what concerned him just as much was that their action in his case was not mirrored in other cases. Those of other faiths within the company were allowed to present visible evidence of their beliefs, including head-dresses, beards and turbans. Equally, WDH involved itself in cultural events and statements which went far beyond their role in housing. The company raised money for war heroes (poppy collection), was registered as an organisation for gay parades, and agreed to holistic alternative therapies being displayed on its website. It even had a slight link with Christianity through carol singing.

As the company had wide interests, Colin felt that no-one could possibly perceive WDH as a "Christian organisation". Displaying the cross in his van was therefore a personal manifestation of faith, one that in no way represented the company's "voice".

A year on from the complaint, in December 2010, WDH amended their van driver policy, stating that "personal displays of any nature in WDH-owned/leased vehicles are not allowed." As a result, Colin was brought before an investigation committee and told formally to remove the cross. "Put it in the glove box" was one suggestion. Threatened with disciplinary action, he was given three days to change his mind. Convinced that the sack awaited, he responded when approached by *The Mail on Sunday* by stating the truth about the whole issue. With huge press attention, he and Geraldine found things difficult at times but were determined not to compromise. With the right to manifest faith at work at stake, Colin was willing to pay the price, in line with his Saviour's sacrifice. The Lord was strengthening him; all he had to do was remain faithful.

In early April 2011, Colin was suspended, pending an

investigation into his involvement with the press. WDH forbade him any contact with the media unless they had sanctioned it. Colin responded by pointing out the public interest and that he was exercising his human rights. Eventually, all signed an agreement which was sanctioned by the CLC.

The following were agreed:

(1) Colin could continue to display the cross on the front of the van dashboard;
(2) There would be no sanction against Colin for speaking to the media;
(3) Colin would return to his normal job at his normal workplace;
(4) Full consultation would take place with work colleagues on his return.

WDH also committed to review its policies and procedures. Colin returned to work, as planned, on 9th May 2011, but discovered that WDH had already reneged on their side of the agreement. Not only was he ostracised by some depot staff, but on return from holiday in June found that he had been moved to a different location, in breach of the agreement. Furthermore, the van he had used for visiting sites, apprentices and colleagues had also been taken away. Advised to use public transport, he was flabbergasted that WDH could ignore a grievance, suspend him when he spoke to the media, and now break the agreement. With his media representations viewed as gross misconduct by bringing the company into disrepute, the company finally dismissed him on 18th August 2011, before his grievance had even been heard.

On advice, Colin decided not to appeal. His situation was then compounded by the Jobcentre in Wakefield refusing him

Jobseekers Allowance, "... due to the circumstances under which my employment ended." He and Geraldine eventually received housing benefits but sadly, on 24th October 2011, she left home, and later filed for divorce. Spending his time over Christmas and New Year 2012 without her, but with family in Scotland, Colin is now alone, but comments that he has a wonderful, loving and healing God to whom he can turn and who still has work for him to do. Colin is also indebted to his biological family in Wakefield and Scotland, along with the wonderful family at Destiny Church and praises God for supplying all his needs and more!

PART TWO

QUESTIONING SAME SEX FOSTERING AND ADOPTING

3

Andrew McClintock
The Magistrate

Andrew was born during the Second World War, near Tonbridge, Kent. Grateful that German bombs narrowly missed the nursing home in which his mother was giving birth to him, he grew up in the Home Counties before graduating from Oxford. Along the way, he joined Voluntary Service Overseas (VSO), which sent him for service in Bechuanaland (later Botswana). This experience was formative. What he learnt from a people who were very different in mindset from the English influenced him greatly in his working life, which began in the Sheffield steel industry in 1967.

Prior to being a student, Andrew had been a churchgoer by habit. In Oxford, however, he attended a lively church which presented him with a fresh version of biblical truth and challenged him to make a personal commitment to Jesus. This decision subsequently influenced his choice of career in manufacturing and industrial relations, and the voluntary work that he and his wife undertook, reaching out to marginalised young people in a coffee bar called the Mustard Seed. In 1980 he took a Master's Degree in Distribution and Logistics, before becoming a self-employed consultant in that new specialism.

It was around this time that Andrew was asked by a friend to consider becoming a Justice of the Peace. Appointment to the magistracy was becoming more open and less secretive than previously, but events did not move apace. He applied and was interviewed but had to wait fully four years for a second interview. On 20th April 1988, he took the judicial oath and began training. Initially involved with lesser criminal cases like shoplifting and drink-driving, further training led him to join the Family Panel. He now encountered issues associated with broken families, e.g. ex-husbands failing to pay upkeep, and mothers refusing fathers access to children, along with requests from local authorities to remove children from their natural families for fostering and adoption.

During the 1990s, court business continued to present the humdrum (serial shoplifters) to the demanding (a police request to urgently remove a child at midnight). This was a time, too, of many changes as political correctness challenged traditional views of marriage, authority and, indeed, right and wrong. One new law – the Human Rights Act 1998 – reflected the UK's growing integration with the European Union. A parallel theme was Equal Opportunities which allowed anyone, even adherents to undemocratic philosophies, to be considered equally with all others applying for a job.

Privately, Andrew was becoming concerned about the changing philosophy of law. When three leading politicians separately accepted invitations to local meetings of the Magistrates Association, he asked each why the government was pressing for laws that favoured intrusive government over individual freedoms, thus undoing the ability of the courts to protect an individual. The answer was broadly and blandly the same – trust the government to get it right.

The lighting of the fuse, which eventually detonated in late 2007, began three years earlier when Parliament was discussing the Civil Partnerships Bill. Clearly, this was to open a door to families headed by two members of the same sex; in time, children for adoption would be recommended by social workers to be placed in such same-sex households. This prospect gave Andrew both moral and practical qualms. It conflicted with his Christian view of divinely-instituted marriage and would probably lead to some emotional lack in children brought up without input from one gender. The Children Act 1989 clearly stated that the priority was always the welfare of the child. With this coming scenario lacking evidence, he was concerned that it was neither legal nor ethical to make the damaged child a guinea pig for research in social science. Conflict was obvious between ignoring the sexuality of the prospective parents and prioritising the child's welfare. With little known of same-sex child nurture, he questioned how a court would handle these conflicting objectives, only to be met with a resounding silence.

The Case

The Bill progressed through Parliament and into law. Andrew's potential dilemma now became imminent. Accordingly, he wrote to the manager of the Court's Family Panel, indicating that he was unwilling to officiate in a case in which a same-sex disposal was in prospect. He would, however, like to remain a member of the Panel for other cases. This letter resulted in a meeting, in January 2006. Surprisingly, present were the Chairman and Secretary of the Lord Chancellor's Advisory Committee. Equally surprisingly, the meeting turned out to be a form of disciplinary hearing as Andrew's request had been seen as a breach of the judicial oath. In essence, he was told that he could not be excused certain cases, having to adjudicate on all cases allotted to him or none. Rather than endorse a regime which he considered led to bad child-nurture, Andrew resigned from the Family Panel on 6th February 2006.

His decision was based on two strands. One, scientific and objective, concerned child welfare. The second, more personal, concerned conscience and the ability to be excused, through religious or moral views, from officiating in processes regarded as wrong. In this way he was no different from conscientious objectors in World War 2, nurses refusing to participate in abortions, or the Muslim pharmacist in Rotherham who refused to supply the morning after pill, in line with the Royal Pharmaceutical Society's ethics code. Andrew felt strongly that in a democracy the law could be upheld whilst being generous enough to excuse individuals from doing what they believed to be wrong. Importantly, he never asserted that a same-sex upbringing was invariably unsuitable; in special circumstances it might prove best for a particular child; nevertheless, a mother + father remained the general starting point.

This might well have been the end of the matter, were it not for several remarkably timed instances, which Andrew ascribed to God's unseen direction of events. Firstly, due to general concern about swelling political correctness, a conference had been arranged by Rob Frost at Cliff College, near Sheffield. There he met Andrea Minichiello Williams, who then represented the Lawyers Christian Fellowship. After listening to her speak, he chatted with her over coffee and was asked whether he had considered challenging the arguments that had led to his resignation. He hadn't, not wishing to embarrass people, but was persuaded that this avoidance of confrontation with a minority PC agenda leads to situations worsening.

Agreeing to be a "bullet in the fight", Andrew needed to know on what technicality he could challenge the refusal of the court's management to accommodate him. His post had been voluntary, with no contract of employment. How could he demonstrate that he had been pushed into a corner where resignation had been forced on him? And would this be interpreted as constructive dismissal? Leaving to work temporarily in Sudan for an NGO called Samaritans' Purse, providing the logistics by which refugees could be supplied with their material needs, on his return home he visited Mark Jones, a lawyer known for human rights cases, and Paul Diamond, a barrister, himself famed for rebutting PC challenges to his own professional behaviour. The decision to work with Paul led to many dealings over the next year and a new friendship.

Andrew spent that summer preparing his case based on issues of conscience, infringement of his human rights and scientific evidence. Together with Andrea, he alerted the Shadow Attorney General, Dominic Grieve, to the importance of resisting these PC developments.

Detonation took place in November 2006. In agreeing to taking a high profile in a publicity campaign organised by Andrea, Andrew was interviewed by *The Sunday Telegraph*. The dam burst, with other newspapers reporting his story, much of it sympathetically, although some were hostile. Many supportive messages encouraged him, although one piece of correspondence from a gay couple made him feel unwell. Nevertheless, he was further encouraged to act after sitting next to a judge at a carol service that Christmas. The judge remarked that he was about to retire, glad that he had not faced a personal issue like Andrew's, and hoping that he would be spared anything like that in his remaining months in office. This disclosure raised the question: how many other professionals who were unhappy with the direction of events simply sit tight, as Andrew had been tempted to do? It reminded him of a lesson he had learnt once in Germany. He and other Sheffield magistrates had visited their counterparts in the steel town of Bochum. On the walls were portraits of past judges. Between 1933 and 1945 there was a notable gap, with no portraits on view, as the system they had administered had not been just.

In 2007, hearings took place at the Employment Tribunal in Sheffield and in the Employment Appeal Tribunal in London. At the first of these, another divinely instigated "coincidence" took place. The media had become very attentive to Roman Catholic adoption agencies, which were threatening to cease work if they were unable to choose mother and father homes. Paul Diamond had located an expert witness, Professor Dean Byrd, a former president of the National Association for Research and Therapy of Homosexuality (NARTH), to testify in support of Andrew. A strong believer in traditional marriage, Professor Byrd argued that from the small amount of evidence available, children could suffer from mother–hunger and father-hunger. Sadly, when it came, the eventual ruling gave little weight to his observations, even though no expert evidence was offered on the other side. Nevertheless, the publicity generated was considerable, with Andrew being stopped in the streets by strangers, including one man who was distraught because his grandchild had been placed in a gay household with contact blocked on the grounds that he had voiced anti-gay sentiments.

While Andrew had much support overall and various invitations to speak, he was surprised that although some church members were forthright in their support, others remained silent for fear of reprisals.

The situation at work was rather different. Of the three hundred-odd magistrates, only eight to ten explicitly voiced their support. Andrew did learn of one who had resigned a year ahead of him on precisely the same grounds, but most made no reference to the issue. Was rocking the boat hard even for those who worked unpaid? He wrote to the Journal of the Magistrates Association, sounding for wider views, but again their non-engagement was deafening. Making contact with a JP elsewhere in the country, he was horrified to discover that that bench had got into trouble simply for raising the matter of the sexuality of the couple receiving the adoptive child. Permission to quote the details of that case was also emphatically refused.

Press comment subsequently died down. His appeal was heard and rejected by the Employment Appeal Tribunal in London, but the trip at least allowed a third divine coincidence to take place. In London, Andrew and his wife visited their daughter, who was a member of Holy Trinity Church, Brompton. The sermon, by The Reverend Nicky Gumbel, was on growing pressure on Christians in the workplace. Introduced to him afterwards, Nicky prayed for his case. God didn't answer this prayer in the way Andrew had hoped, as Paul Diamond's appeal on his behalf was blocked from going to the Court of Appeal. Legally, this was the end of the road for Andrew, but his stand was not entirely in vain.

Andrew discovered through his cousin, a leading solicitor in personnel law, that the tribunal ruling in his case was often referred to in employment disputes. He also learnt that other cases of apparent religious discrimination (or of rights suppressed) at work have entered the legal system, with several cases currently under consideration by the European Court of Human Rights in Strasbourg. All being well, it may be that between them they will pave the way for other Christians in the UK to express their conscience more freely at work in the future.

On reflection, Andrew concludes that his case affected him less than others detailed in this book. His role as a JP had been voluntary, neither contractual nor paid, and although he had to drop his work with the Family Panel, he has been able to continue with criminal adjudications. His livelihood had not been at stake, but it was still a sad way to end his family work on the bench.

Now retired and out of office, he remains concerned for the true victims here – those disadvantaged children who have been taken into homes he would deem less than fully desirable. Moreover, having had his eyes opened through the shabby treatment he received, he now spends time informing others of the undesirable consequences of PC behaviour. The bottom line is that he wishes to encourage other followers of Jesus to challenge second-class treatment of individuals who cannot stand up for themselves – a very positive way to end.

4

Sheila Matthews
The Community Paediatrician

Sheila was born and grew up in Glasgow and qualified as a doctor from the university in her home town in 1981. Two years later she took up a short-term job in Northamptonshire, intending to move on again afterward – but meeting her husband in a church group, and then marriage, changed those plans. She initially settled in general practice, but the birth of a small, very hungry daughter, in addition to on-call and night visits, led her to move into community paediatrics in 1991. The aim was to remain in this speciality for a year, but such short-termism proved too modest; Sheila would spend the next two decades working in this area of medicine.

Community paediatrics is about supporting children and families with special needs. Sheila enjoyed the challenges involved and her desire to provide the best service possible led her to gain a distinction in an M.Sc. in her speciality, and to become involved in adoption and fostering. At her very first adoption training meeting she was asked to define herself in three words and chose "Christian, doctor and mother." Had she been allowed more words, she would have chosen "wife, daughter, sister and friend" because she believes relationships shape us and our society.

Her work in adoption and fostering grew, and with the retirement of the previous Medical Advisor in 2004 she was appointed by Northamptonshire County Council as Medical

Advisor for adoption and fostering and a member of the Adoption Panel. The two roles are linked, but different.

The Medical Advisor's job is to advise Social Services of any health issues in adults applying to foster or adopt, and in the children being assessed for adoption or long-term fostering. In addition to understanding the adoption process thoroughly, Sheila was very aware of the unique behavioural, developmental and physical needs of this group of children, which enabled her to contribute much to the assessment process and to become an advocate for these vulnerable individuals.

Her role within the Adoption Panel was rather different. Along with other Panel members, her responsibility was to vote on whether to approve prospective adoptive parents and how to match them with specific children.

Ever since taking on this new post in 2004, Sheila had two roles. Firstly, she continued to work as a community paediatrician employed by Northamptonshire NHS PCT. Her adoption work was interwoven with these other duties and was done for the county council, focused on the cases identified by social services. The arrangement was a little complicated, but as her adoption duties were specifically performed for the county council, it would later be ruled that she was employed by that body from the perspective of employment legislation.

Central to her role in adoption and fostering was the production of detailed and accurate reports on the children involved. To achieve this, Sheila collated health information available from other sources in order to best understand and make appropriate recommendations concerning their future needs. She also commented on the health examinations of prospective adopters and foster carers carried out by their own GPs. When appropriate, she would meet with them to gain further information about their health. Although occasionally an individual was unsuitable on health grounds, more often it was about ensuring they addressed any health issues, received support and were realistic about what they could cope with. Information or discussions about their sexuality did not often arise in this context, but one thing was paramount: Sheila's primary interest was always that the best match for each child should take place.

To achieve this she discussed cases regularly with a wide range of professionals, including social workers. They have a very difficult job and she hugely respected those she worked with, knowing how hard they worked to make fair assessments and to encourage and support prospective carers. She was able to contribute to this process by introducing new ideas in some areas, with regular evening meetings taking place in which potential adopters could meet as a group, hear about children awaiting placement and find out more about the children they were interested in.

Overall, Sheila felt that the Adoption Service in North-amptonshire was excellent, with much work going on before children arrived at the Panel to be recommended for adoption, and before adopters were presented for approval. This was crucial, for decisions made by adopters, social workers and the Panel have far-reaching implications for the lives of the children and their new families.

A pivotal point in the adoption process was the Panel meeting. Panel members range in experience from social workers and local councillors to parents with adopted children, and others interested in adoption or familiar with working with children. In addition to these voting members there are non-voting members present, including a legal advisor and an adoption advisor. In total, ten very different people sit round the table, as broad a representation as possible. The amount of paperwork is vast, and there is much to discuss as members mention their concerns and formulate a list of questions for the social workers and applicants. They are then interviewed by the Panel, with any health-related issues being explained to the other members by the Medical Advisor. Prospective adopters find this part of the proceedings very nerve-wracking, having to answer questions from a large number of people, all looking at them and making notes! They are very keen to make a good impression so they can move on to the next stage. After the interview, applicants wait outside during the discussion.

Voting then takes place. Each panel member votes either to approve the application of couples to be adopters or on the match of a specific child with approved adopters. The Panel's recommendation is then passed to the Head of Services for Children and Young People for Northamptonshire County Council. This person takes into account the discussion and recommendation of the Panel but is not bound by them; in making the final decision, the Head of Services is known as the Decision Maker.

The Issue

In March 2004, Sheila attended the council's training for Panel Members on Gay, Lesbian and Bisexual Parenting. As a general principle, she feels it is important to listen carefully to people and to consider other opinions with an open mind. So having a different viewpoint from the presenters did not prevent her from considering what they were saying, and she found the day very informative and thought-provoking. Over the next few years she continued to think deeply about this issue, not wishing to discriminate positively or negatively without good reason. In studying research and opinions from different sources, however, she became aware that there was evidence that children placed with same sex couples did less well. Sheila was aware that this was a contentious issue, with a diverse range of views, but she knew a large proportion of people shared her concerns.

In her position as a voting Panel member, Sheila understood that legislation permitted same sex couples to adopt, and that indeed they are positively encouraged to apply; nevertheless, whilst not considering herself to be homophobic, and happy to mix with homosexual individuals, whether they be patients, colleagues or friends, her concerns about children growing up in homosexual households remained. She became aware that the homosexual lifestyle carries higher risks of physical and mental health problems, and that living in a same sex household influences children towards becoming homosexual themselves. Also, children do better with mother and father role models and influences in their lives. She discussed these findings with a number of other doctors and researchers, and read widely. In this context, Patricia Morgan's book *Children as Trophies?* proved to be a very helpful review of the research available up to 2002. It confirmed Sheila's personal Christian belief that marriage between a man and a woman in a faithful monogamous sexual relationship is the most appropriate environment for the upbringing of children.

Sheila was obliged by her profession and by the Children Act 1989 to act in the best interests and welfare of a child. In practice, this meant as a Panel member she had to answer one question: Do you believe that this particular placement is in the child's best interests? It was a big question and one she took seriously, for the issues under consideration went well beyond health; they encompassed the adopting parents' lifestyle, social environment, support networks and coping ability – anything which might impact on their ability to parent. Much to consider and get right if the child was to be placed in a good family which could met their needs now and in the future. The more she thought about it, the more she realised that a personal lifestyle choice is one thing for an individual, but a very different matter when it involves children growing up in that environment, particularly where significant disadvantage and disruption has already taken place. Furthermore, if she believed that the Bible is God's Word, she could not simply ignore teaching which she found "inconvenient".

God's rules for living are there for our benefit, not to make us miserable. And whilst it is right to listen to others' points of view, ultimately the Bible is the source of Truth. Homosexual practice is not part of God's design for our lives and there are consequences, should we choose to live life that way.

Faced with a clear choice, when the moment came, her mind was made up.

The Case

In 2007, Sheila participated at a Panel when an application from a same sex couple was heard. She presented the health information without bias, but discreetly abstained from voting on the recommendation because of her position on the suitability of same sex couples as adoptive parents. She hoped by acting in this way she would not influence other Panel members (who were not aware of her views) or cause distress to the applicants. Her action did not affect the final outcome for the couple, for this was the job of the Decision Maker, but would allow her to contribute to the Panel without compromising her integrity.

In January 2009, the issue arose again and Sheila asked to abstain from voting. She was advised not to attend the case and was later invited to meet with the senior social managers for the council. The meeting took place on 22nd April 2009, and the issues raised by her request were discussed. A week later she received a letter from the Head of Services stating that she should be replaced as Panel Medical Advisor on the grounds that they could not have a Panel member who was not prepared to consider all applications on their merits; they could also not allow her to abstain from voting because of the council's commitment to equality and diversity policies and because the law allowed same sex couples to adopt.

Sheila found the decision extraordinary. Not only did the council blatantly ignore evidence from rational scientific research, but also her experience and commitment to the job. Furthermore, she only sought to abstain from voting in these circumstances, which amounted to fewer than one in twenty cases. In no way had she attempted to influence other Panel members or to discriminate against individual couples by raising these issues in Panel discussions. Any discrimination, instead, seemed to be against her, on the grounds of religion and belief.

In June 2009, she challenged the decision in a letter to the Corporate Director for Children and Young People for the County Council. Seven weeks later she received a reply, stating that the Council agreed that she could continue to attend Panel as Medical Advisor until the end of July 2009, when another doctor would be appointed to replace her.

Although regretting the decision, Sheila felt that this was a reasonable compromise and intended to carry on doing assessments and coordinating the process whilst liaising with the incoming Panel doctor. But it would not work out this way.

In July the new doctor was appointed by the PCT and Council as Medical Advisor, as planned. Sheila tried to fit in with the new arrangements, but her time allocated for adoption work was reduced, and she was effectively sidelined. The system she had developed and which was working well was ignored, and the quality of the service slipped. It became increasingly difficult to work under these circumstances, and then her reports were undermined and her recommendations questioned.

A particular case arose and she discussed it in detail with the social workers involved, reaching an agreement on the recommendations. Later, she was stunned to learn that the individual applicant had rejected her report, without seeing it, on the grounds of their homosexuality. This had not been a factor in the report at all and she would have expected the social workers to have continued to be in full agreement with what she had said. Instead, another report was requested from a colleague and her work which had taken many hours was simply discarded. Not only was she not told about this but the flow of information about other cases and Panel decisions also ceased. Finally, she was not even informed when the other doctor would miss Panel meetings, even though it had previously been agreed she would stand in.

At this point she realised that she could no longer work in this environment, but she was not prepared to give up the adoption work and expand into other areas of community paediatrics. Why should she? The only reason she had been moved was due to her request to abstain. There had never been any question about the quality of her work, a point reflected in her appraisals which had always been good.

Up to now, adoption work had always given her great satisfaction; it allowed her to put together her adult skills (gleaned from general practice) with those from paediatrics. Enthusiastic, and more than prepared to go the extra mile for the children for whom she felt personally responsible, she had willingly spent evenings and weekends preparing reports, and regularly passed on her knowledge to junior doctors in the local hospital paediatric department.

Now, with her role limited through no fault of her own, her *joie de vivre* and drive had taken a big hit. She met with NHS managers on several occasions to attempt to resolve her situation, but left feeling increasingly frustrated. She had hoped that after nineteen years' service the organisation would support her, but instead, she felt isolated, undervalued and demeaned as the managers dismissively ignored her excellent performance records and manoeuvred to diminish her adoption role further. The result was that she began to lose self-esteem and confidence in her ability, and eventually she became so demoralised that she felt she had no option but to resign from her job in community paediatrics.

Reflecting on what had taken place, it was clear that her dismissal by the council and treatment by the PCT occurred solely due to her stance on same sex parenting. As this reflected her religious beliefs on sexual ethics, it seemed that people of faith were expected to set aside their beliefs when working for governmental organisations. This seemed particularly strange when those same ethical beliefs were not so long ago promoted by the same organisations.

To her mind, such silencing was quite unnecessary. With only a small proportion of cases involving same sex adoption, it should have been perfectly possible for her to abstain from voting in these few cases, thus reasonably accommodating her beliefs whilst allowing her to act in the lead role of Medical Advisor to the Panel. After all, other voting members were allowed to abstain if there was a conflict of interest in a particular case.

Having resigned, Sheila knew that that she would find it difficult to get another job in community paediatrics. Taking a deep breath, she decided to retrain in general practice. Not sure if she could do it after a gap of twenty years, she sat exams and joined a practice under supervision, loving the experience and thoroughly enjoying being back with patients of all ages in a supportive environment. After some temporary jobs, she now works permanently in one practice. The road has been rocky, but God has been good, and she has absolutely no regrets about making a stand or leaving her former job. She felt very humbled that people all over the world, as well as personal friends, took trouble to contact her to express disbelief at what had happened and to support her stance. She remains very grateful to all those who have backed her along the way with prayer, advice, a listening ear and encouragement. Included within their number was the Christian Medical Fellowship (CMF) and the team from the CLC.

When she received the Council's letter dismissing her from the Panel, Sheila contacted the CMF who directed her to the CLC. Andrea, Paul Diamond and the team attended meetings with her but also made her aware that what had taken place was not simply an isolated incident but was happening to Christians all over Britain who took their faith seriously, but whose rights and beliefs were being trumped by those of other groups, e.g. homosexuals. It was important to act, so with the support of the CLC she referred the matter to an employment tribunal. Her claim against Northamptonshire County Council was on the basis that she had been dismissed due to religious discrimination which contravened Articles 10 and 21 of the Charter of Fundamental Rights of the European Union (2000).

All Sheila wanted when she presented her case in November 2010 was an acknowledgement that she should not have been dismissed. Suspecting that she had been discriminated against not only through her faith convictions but also because of her professional views, she presented a summary of the research evidence about outcomes for children and the risks of the homosexual lifestyle, alongside biblical quotes. The judge, however, decided that as her views were held by a number of groups of people, some with faith and others without, there was therefore no religious discrimination, and that anyone holding her views would be dismissed. Sheila felt he had made his mind up before the start and was simply not prepared to consider the wider issues.

CLC barrister Paul Diamond, asked for her case to be referred to the European Court of Justice, in order to examine how different rights could be accommodated without disadvantaging one group. The request was refused. Nevertheless, her case has raised the issue of the "right to work" in government bodies – for Christians and others with strong beliefs. The law needs to protect people of faith from discrimination arising from current political ideology, which led to the county council choosing to lose a highly skilled professional, with all the attendant waste of experience and training, rather than accommodate her faith. Vulnerable children could then have been protected rather than being placed in jeopardy in the name of political correctness.

With legal redress seemingly barred, Sheila has managed to raise the issues in a wider forum by giving a number of newspaper, television and radio interviews. This was not easy, but pleasingly it generated much debate, not just around the rights of Christians to live in accordance with their beliefs but – also importantly – about the best environments for children to grow up in. Hopefully this will encourage others to stand up for what they believe is right.

Throughout her case, Sheila makes pains to state that she is no victim, even though what happened to her was unfair, unnecessary and had a profound effect on her career. She has received some offensive personal comment through the media coverage, and was sad that those people chose not to engage in reasonable, respectful debate. Something that gets lost in all this talk of discrimination against Christians is that they actually seek the best for others. It is not about judging or excluding others, but about pointing them to a better, more fulfilling way of living.

Sheila did not want to lose the job she so enjoyed, but firmly believes that God puts us in places for a purpose and that He is trustworthy. The experience has made her think about what was most important to her, and to realise that to trust God you have to step out, not knowing what the outcome will be – exciting, even if sometimes scary!

But it has not been easy. To help her understand why she should have become involved with the debate on homosexual issues, someone quoted Martin Luther: "If I profess with loudest voice and clearest exposition every portion of the truth of God except that little point which the world and the devil are at that moment attacking, I am not confessing Christ. Where the battle rages, there the loyalty of the soldier is proved, and to be steady on all the battlefield besides, is mere flight and disgrace if he flinches at that point."

Although she would not have chosen to have gone through this experience, it has proved to be her battleground. In standing, she has learnt more about God, and that whatever happens in the future, her life is in His hands.

5

Eunice and Owen Johns
The Foster Parents

Eunice and Owen are a late middle-aged African-Caribbean couple, who emigrated from Jamaica in the 1960s. Eunice had been brought up in a strong Christian family and was the youngest of ten children. Attendance at church was mandatory, but no problem for her as she graduated from the choir to become a youth leader in due course. She also enjoyed school, but at fifteen was sent to London to live with an older sister. Emigration was accepted as the norm and, although initially homesick, the outgoing and sociable teenager enjoyed the new experiences and made some African-Caribbean friends in her comprehensive school in Brixton.

She left school without formal qualifications but was accepted by a nursing school in Derby, which meant she could live close to many of her brothers. Quickly deciding, however, that she was not ready to be a nurse, she instead obtained employment in the catering department at Rolls Royce, and then as a machinist. It was here that she met Owen He had emigrated from Jamaica a couple of years previously, having been brought up on a small farm by his mother after his father died when he was five. He too had been happy and secure as a child, although strict discipline compelled him to work on the farm at either end of his school day as well as looking after younger siblings. As for

Eunice, churchgoing and a strong moral code was part of his upbringing. Some time after his mother remarried he had decided to emigrate, aged seventeen, and was determined to make something of himself. Ignoring racism and rejection by potential employers, he worked on a poultry farm, then mixed paints, before being taken on at Rolls Royce initially as a labourer, later becoming a metal polisher. Apart from a short period away from the firm in the 1980s, he has worked there ever since.

The couple married in 1969. Owen continued in his steady job, whilst Eunice combined motherhood with a succession of part-time jobs before starting to train again as a nurse, in 1975. Qualifying as an SEN specialising in geriatrics, she worked nights to fit in with family responsibilities and found the job to be fulfilling. However, she disliked the increasing bureaucracy and was eventually relieved to retire on health grounds, due to arthritis of the neck.

Socially, the couple had become very established, living in a bungalow on a private estate in Derby, surrounded by their large extended family of four children, six grandchildren and one great grandchild, together with friends they see frequently.

Spiritually, Eunice and Owen are members of the Pentecostal Church in Village Street, Derby, and their Christian faith underpins everything they do. They have always been believers, but more recently, they (separately) became "born again", since when the depth of their faith and their church activity has increased markedly. Although not formally employed by the church, Eunice's commitment sees her in church every day bar Saturday. On Sundays she coordinates the Sunday School, attending the service herself in the evening.

The Johns are therefore committed Christians who have always loved the company of children, not only within their family but also at church. Being involved with children ("it's what they do") has been noted by adult referees, who describe their relationships with children, and management skills, as good. A natural extension of this gift was to become involved in fostering.

As potential short-term foster carers, the Johns were aware that relatively few of the children they might look after would share their Christian lifestyle. In an interview with a social worker, the couple stated that they would never try to compel a child to become a Christian and would be very conscious that the child's parents or main carers might be atheist, or of a different faith, and might therefore be uncomfortable if they felt the child was being influenced in any way. The only indication a child would have of their beliefs would be the presence of Bibles and saying grace at mealtimes. Prayers were otherwise said privately, and there were no other obviously religious articles around the house. They would, however, always answer a child's questions honestly if appropriate, and, with the consent of their carers or parents, children could accompany them to church.

Not surprisingly, the Johns feel that their strong moral code would benefit society enormously if more widely shared. Their beliefs may be summarised as a return to "older" values, in which young people respect their elders and where family life, based on heterosexual relationships, was the bedrock of society and the only acceptable pattern. They are aware that their own offspring may not subscribe entirely to this pattern, but while visiting they always show respect, and abide by the couple's wishes and preferences.

The Case

Mr and Mrs Johns started to foster children in Derbyshire in August 1992. Over the next year, they fostered a number of children on a short-term basis, offering a safe and secure home and guided especially by Eunice's Christian faith. But in 1994 they opened a Caribbean restaurant, which put paid to fostering as it gave them insufficient time to devote to the children in their care. Formally, however, they were registered as carers with Derby City Council until January 1995.

Nine years later, in 2004, the couple decided to give up the restaurant and re-applied to Derby City Council. However, other personal and professional commitments led them to withdraw from the process, and Owen resumed full-time work at Rolls Royce. In June 2006, they again expressed interest in short-term fostering and formally applied to the Council in January 2007. By now the Johns considered themselves able and resourced to provide the necessary care and support for foster children. They were assessed by an independent social worker, whose conclusions were as follows:

Both Eunice and Owen expressed strong views on homosexuality, stating that it is "against God's laws and morals". These views stemmed from their religious convictions and beliefs. Eunice explained at a later interview that she'd always been brought up to believe that having a different sexual orientation was unnatural and wrong, and that these convictions had not come about as a result of her being 'saved'.

The Johns were then asked whether they would be able to

support a young person who was confused about his or her sexuality. Giving what was seen as a negative answer, Eunice mentioned a visit she had made to San Francisco which was not enjoyable, for the city had many gay inhabitants which made her feel uncomfortable. The Johns were also recorded as stating that they would not be able to take a child to a mosque. Nevertheless, Eunice and Owen always made it clear that they would love any child that came into their care, no matter what their sexual orientation.

The social worker was concerned about the Johns' views and discussed them with the Manager of the Fostering Team. Further interviews were deemed necessary, using the Fostering Standards as a basis for discussion. However, if there seemed to be no perceptible movement towards their accepting the Standards on Valuing Diversity, they would be advised to withdraw their application.

In August 2007, the social worker met with Eunice Johns alone. Expressing her concerns, she regarded their views on homosexuality as not equating with various aspects of the Fostering Standards, notably:

- The need to value diversity;
- Addressing a child's needs in relation to their sexuality;
- Enhancing a child's feelings of self-worth;
- Helping a child deal with all forms of discrimination.

In summary, she emphasised the need for carers to value people regardless of their sexual orientation. Eunice responded by saying that she did value people as individuals and would be able to support a young person on that basis. Furthermore, she had stayed with her nephew, who was gay and lived with his partner in the US, and treated them no differently from anyone else. Nevertheless, she would not compromise her beliefs.

Eunice was then presented with four possible scenarios. How would she support a young person who:

- Was confused about their sexuality and thinks they may be gay?
- Is being bullied at school regarding their sexual orientation?
- Bullies others regarding the above?
- Whose parents are gay?

According to the social worker, Eunice's response to the first situation was that she would support any child, but did not explain how she would go about this. In regard to the second situation, Eunice would reassure the child and tell them to ignore the bullying. In the third case, Eunice was not sure what to do, but would work at it; in the fourth, gay parents wouldn't matter, for she would work with anyone. Hypothetical situations, but ones which were used to judge the Owens.

The social worker's main concern was that both Eunice and Owen took a superficial approach to helping children of a different ethnicity and sexuality to deal with abuse and discrimination. Based on their own experiences, Eunice and Owen believed the best approach was to ignore abuse and make the best of yourself, not appreciating how abuse affected the self-esteem of looked-after children. The social worker felt that training would help them in this regard, but she was concerned that they had not drawn on their previous experience as carers. She also expressed concern about the time they could give to caring – Owen worked five to six days a week and Eunice remained very involved with church affairs. This was another smokescreen. When asked whether each would be willing to attend church on alternate Sundays, neither wished to compromise, but would take any child with them. In concluding, the professional's advice was that the couple withdraw their application.

The next day, Eunice telephoned the social worker, informing her that they wished to place these issues before the Fostering Panel for discussion. In addition, they wished to change to another social worker, as Eunice felt that the advice not to foster was given because she was a Christian. This the social worker denied, but would not debate further over the telephone. It was agreed that a Panel date would be arranged, but prior to that the social worker and her manager would visit the Johns.

The purpose of this joint visit was explicitly stated: due to the concerns already expressed, the two of them hoped that the Johns would agree to withdraw their application. The manager began by stressing that their views did not equate with valuing individuals equally or promoting diversity, nor had the Johns acknowledged that their strong beliefs would probably adversely affect their ability to support a young person with confused sexual identity. Eunice disagreed, disputing that she had ever said that she couldn't support anyone with such difficulties; her beliefs would not affect her ability to care. In reality, she felt the two professionals were saying that they could not foster because they were Christians.

The professionals did concede, however, that the Johns had made arrangements for Sunday mornings. Their son, Kevin, had agreed to look after any child for the three hours they spent in church. How very sad that the council was putting a condition down that children should not attend church.

The Panel met in November 2007 and considered the social worker's report. Stating that, "the department needs to be careful not to appear to discriminate against them on religious grounds," it continued, "the issue has not arisen just because of their religion as there are homophobic people that are non-Christian. The ability to promote diversity is the main issue."

The Johns then addressed the Panel. Eunice spoke first, referring to press coverage of a pastor who had had a foster child removed from his care because of similar issues. Asserting again that she would not compromise her religious beliefs, she continued, "I will love and respect, no matter what sexuality ... but I cannot tell a child it is OK to be homosexual. Then you will not be able to trust me. There has got to be different ways of going through this without having to compromise my faith." Mr Johns then told the Panel that documents regarding diversity had changed from when they fostered previously. Mrs Johns equally accepted that society has changed, but stressed that there must be a way where she did not need to compromise and say it is OK to be gay.

Following the meeting, the Panel understood that conflict between the fostering guidelines and their personal beliefs meant that the Johns had amicably withdrawn from the process and wrote to them, closing the application. In this, they were mistaken. Instead, having come across Andrea Williams through Revelation TV, working on behalf of another Christian couple (Vince and Pauline Matherick), the Johns had already contacted the Christian Legal Centre for similar assistance.

In February 2008, Paul Diamond drafted a letter on their behalf, informing the city council that they had not withdrawn their application and wished to pursue it. The letter also expressed concern that the council considered their Christian faith and biblical beliefs about sexual orientation prevented them from being suitable foster carers.

In late February 2008, the Johns gave a number of interviews to the local and national press. Media coverage had been co-ordinated by Andrea Williams and led to the council rapidly reinstating their application. In writing to the Johns, however, the council still recognised that their views on homosexual relationships presented a "fundamental difficulty", but reiterated that the Panel's recommendation "was not due to your religious beliefs". This was not how Eunice and Owen saw things. They wrote back, asking for clarification on whether people who hold orthodox views on sexual ethics are suitable to be foster carers. In reply, the council declined to answer this question. In a further attempt at clarification, and by now somewhat exasperated by the lack of transparency in policy, the Johns suggested to the council that compromising religious beliefs appeared to be essential. Furthermore, the couple viewed the council's failure to answer their question as a sign that they were not prepared to deny that those holding orthodox views are viewed as "homophobic" by the council. Such a description demeaned and degraded their faith and dignity.

In July 2008, the council replied that it had no policy "which states that Christians can only foster if they compromise their views on sexual ethics" – a general answer, but inadequate, with practical questions remaining. Further communication from the Johns received a similar answer which again denied any form of religious discrimination.

Not put off, the Johns had already applied again to be foster carers. The new application process allowed them to meet another social worker, who produced a forty-eight page report six months later. In it, she concluded that the Johns were kind and hospitable, do their best to make a child welcome and comfortable, respond sensitively to the child and take their responsibilities as carers seriously. Nevertheless, she had reservations that they would meet the council's expectations, and thus had difficulty in recommending them for approval as mainstream foster carers. She did feel, however, that the Panel might consider them in situations where children match a specific profile, where demands and difficulties should be less intense. However, even in less challenging roles, she queried whether the usual level of insight and skill shouldn't remain a requirement. The difficulty, as ever, concerned their unchanging view on same sex relationships.

Eunice received a copy of the report before the Panel met. Unhappy that once more it seemed to be inconclusive, the Johns asked a further time for clarification on policy. The Panel met in March 2009 and deferred a decision. In response, Paul, Andrea and the Johns agreed with Derby City Council that a joint declaration be sought from the High Court in relation to Derby City Council's position regarding Christians with traditional views of sexual ethics, their suitability to foster and whether people can go through fostering application without discrimination. The relevant UK government ministries were informed of the proceedings, but declined to intervene, but the Equality and Human Rights Commission applied to take part and was given permission to do so in October 2010.

The hearing took place the following month. What proceeded was described in the official judgment as "most unusual." In addition to the documents provided by both sides, the Equality and Human Rights Commission provided a witness statement by its interim Director of Legal Enforcement. The intention was to explain the impact of views opposed to, or disapproving of, same sex lifestyles on the development and well-being of children and young people, including those of gay and lesbian orientation. Indeed, the Commission had produced over 200 pages of literature on this issue. By way of response, Mr Diamond referred to a plethora of other research, mainly from North America, characterising the material relied on by the Commission as highly controversial, selective and not accepted by experts in the field.

The court was clearly in no position to evaluate the information presented, lacking both the expertise and the number of days required to do so. They agreed with Mr Diamond that these were issues for Parliament or other policy makers. Instead, the court focused on the question posed by the claimants and for which they sought an answer: how does the Local Authority as a Fostering Agency balance the obligations owed under the Equality Act 2006 (no discrimination through religion or belief) with those owed under the Equality Act 2007 (no discrimination based on sexual orientation)? Notwithstanding these obligations, the Local Authority was also subject to the Human Rights Act 1998, whilst applying the criteria within the National Minimum Standards for Fostering Services and Derby City Council's Fostering Policy when deciding whether to approve potential foster carers. The punchline was obvious: in such a complex balancing exercise, did the Local Authority have a duty to treat the welfare of its looked-after children as its paramount consideration?

In order to focus thoughts, shortly before the hearing each party was asked to state exactly what declaration they sought. The claimants stated the following:

- All persons adhering to a traditional code of sexual ethics (i.e. any sexual union outside marriage – understood as a lifelong relationship of fidelity between a man and a woman – is morally undesirable) should not be considered unsuitable to be foster carers for this reason alone;
- Persons who attend church services at a mainstream denomination are, in principle, suitable to be foster carers;

- It is unlawful for a Foster Service to ask potential foster carers their views on homosexuality in the absence of the needs of a specific child;
- It is unlawful for a public authority to describe religious adherents who adhere to a moral code of sexual ethics as "homophobic".

By contrast, the declaration sought by the defendant was that the fostering service provider may be acting lawfully in deciding not to approve a prospective foster carer where there is antipathy or disapproval of homosexuality and same sex relationships, along with an inability to respect and positively value the same.

Mr Diamond, when granted turn to speak, introduced the wider issue of religion and the law. Concerning religious freedoms, he questioned whether the advancement of gay rights was beginning to threaten religious liberty. Asserting that the modern British state was "ill-suited to serve as an ethical authority", he complained that it is seeking to force Christian believers "into the closet". Identifying the issue before the court as "whether a Christian couple are fit and proper persons to foster (and, by implication, to adopt), he also asked the court to consider "whether Christian (and Jewish and Muslim) views on sexual ethics are worthy of respect in a democratic society". He went on to submit that what is being contended for is a blanket ban on all Christians (and, indeed, all persons of faith) from being foster parents in the UK, through established public policy which views the majority of world religions as bigoted or discriminatory, because their beliefs include a code of sexual ethics that requires sexual expression to be between a man and a woman.

It is fair to say that the court did not take kindly to Mr Diamond's arguments! Describing his views as a travesty of reality, the judgment denied that Christians (or, for that matter, Jews or Muslims) were not "fit and proper" persons to foster or adopt; there was no blanket ban sought, nor was Christianity or any other faith being "de-legitimised". Christians were not being forced into the closet, they were not bigots and possessed no second-class status. Instead, fundamentally everyone is equal before the law and entitled to dignity and respect.

The court then pronounced further on religion and homosexuality. Mr Diamond had argued that "all of the major religions (Judaism, Christianity and Islam) teach against homosexual conduct", and that, "all hold to the orthodox view that any sexual union outside marriage between one man and one woman is morally undesirable", marriage being a lifelong fidelity between the same. To these propositions, the court took exception, citing that whilst the Sharia is still understood in many places as making homosexuality a capital offence, the Church of England permits its clergy, as long as they remain celibate, to enter into civil partnerships. Moreover, the Christian view of marriage, espoused by Mr Diamond, hardly accords with the Sharia permitting a man to have up to four wives, any of whom he could divorce unilaterally. In summary, the court emphasised the principles regulating the relationship between the law and religion, and that we live in a democratic and pluralist society, not a theocracy.

The judgment went on to examine the relationship between religion and the law in the UK. Starting with the law, the court noted that this country, historically, had been part of the Christian West, with an established Christian church remaining. However, enormous changes in social and religious life over the last century have led, paradoxically, to both increased secularity and a multi-cultural community of many diverse faiths. As secular judges serving this multi-cultural community, they were bound to "do right to all manner of people ... without fear or favour, affection or ill will." Christianity was not referred to in any laws of the realm, with the aphorism, "Christianity is part of the common law of England" deemed mere rhetoric, at least since a judgment made in 1917 made it impossible to contend that it is law.

Moreover, since the late 1700s, marriage was predominantly a civil contract; the sacred and spiritual aspects had been "obliterated", although some still considered it a religious vow.

The court now turned its attention to religion. Religion, whatever the faith, was no doubt to be encouraged, but was not the business of the government or the secular courts. The court would, naturally, respect and give weight to an individual's religious principles, as demanded by Article 9 of the European Convention. Nevertheless, in doing so, the law took an essentially neutral view of religious beliefs, benevolently tolerating cultural and religious diversity. Secular judges were wary of crossing the divide between church and state, would not weigh one religion against another and, recognising that all religions demanded equal respect, would pass no judgment on religious beliefs held by one particular section of society. Finally, civil courts would not adjudicate on purely religious issues or controversies. This was long understood, as was the fact that that "religious belief, no matter how conscientiously held or how ancient or respectable the religion, could never immunise the believer from the reach of the secular law."

Having reminded all involved of the general principles, the court now became more specific. Some cultural beliefs have been regulated if deemed contrary to a child's welfare; corporal punishment was an example. Equally, certain religious practices had fallen foul of public policy, with examples given in relation to Islam and Judaism. Tension between religious and secular laws resulted, with the dispute presently before the court seen in these terms. In fact, the Johns' was merely one of a number of recent cases in which tension existed between an individual's Christian belief and discrimination law enacted by Parliament.

In case anyone was in any doubt, the court then made its position abundantly clear by referring to a comment by Lord Hope, made in relation to another recent discrimination case. He held that civil authorities had no right to interfere in the spiritual government and jurisdiction of the church; equally, where two parties enter into a contract binding in civil law, they were then under the jurisdiction of civil courts, which would not regard any possible discrimination as a spiritual matter.

The court then made reference to Article 9 of the European Convention on Human Rights, in which the right to manifest religion, both publicly and privately, is subject to legal limitations where necessary in the interests of public safety, including the protection of the rights and freedoms of others. With these preliminary matters dealt with, the court now looked at the legal matters of issue between the Johns and Derby City Council.

Mr Diamond's arguments on behalf of the claimants were essentially that the Johns' Christian beliefs should not have been considered in their application as their views on sexuality are not a legitimate fostering concern. Secondly, the council's position was contrary to Article 9 of the Convention and thus constituted religious discrimination. And lastly, it is unreasonable for the majority of the population to be excluded from possible fostering because of its Christian beliefs.

The defendant's barrister, in turn, noted that Mr Diamond had not challenged the council's policies, merely the way they were applied. He also submitted that if the council did not approve foster carers who objected to homosexuality and same sex relationships, it would be acting consistently and lawfully. The Equality Commissioner then stated as a generality that, "there is often scope for change where a person is willing to perform his or her professional duties in a way required by applicable standards, notwithstanding personal belief." She added that, "attitudes too might be changed, moderated or modified through training, counselling and support."

By now, it was clear which way the wind was blowing. Further legal discussion concerning discrimination took place before the court returned to the Johns' case. The issues at stake were precisely the three placed before the court by Mr Diamond.

The court ruled that the policies set out in the National Minimum Standards for Fostering emphasised the need to value diversity, promote equality and to treat children non-judgmentally, regardless of their sexual orientation or preference; this duty applied not only to the child but to the child's parents and wider family, any of whom could be homosexual. In these circumstances, it was quite impossible for a local authority not to consider a prospective foster carer's views on sexuality as it might affect their behaviour and treatment of any child being fostered by them.

Secondly, the question of any religious discrimination was tackled. The court had to decide whether the Johns' application had been turned down because of their stance on sexuality or because of their religious beliefs. Only in the latter case would religious discrimination apply. Taking into account both the fostering standards and Article 9, which provides only "qualified" rights to manifest religion in practice, the court discounted any discrimination on religious grounds. Mr Diamond's third concern was similarly discounted after the court looked again at the evidence presented.

Furthermore, when the local Panel in Derbyshire re-considered the Johns' application in February 2012, the issue of diversity remained at the core of their decision again not to approve them as carers. The case was lost, but the struggle continues, albeit at a snail's pace. An application has been made to the European Court of Human Rights, and now that decisions have been made in relation to the four other Christian cases, including Chaplin (Chapter 1) and McFarlane (Chapter 6), the CLC is now free to pursue justice for the Johns in this chamber later in 2013.

PART THREE

COUNSELLING AND SAME SEX ISSUES

6

Gary McFarlane
The Relationship Counsellor

Gary was born in Jamaica in 1961 and lived there with his sisters throughout his early childhood. His parents, however, lived in England during this time and it wasn't until 1967 that Gary and his sisters joined them in the UK. This was effectively the first time they had met and linking up as a family was not entirely successful. Gary never re-bonded with his parents, growing up a quiet, shy, reserved child, a loner.

The four children grew up in Bristol. At secondary school, Gary felt stereotyped by teachers due to his colour. "O" levels were considered beyond him and so an ambition to join the Navy by gaining "O" level passes was considered to be too high an aspiration. Consequently, he did not view himself as intelligent, but he was prepared to study hard. Catching up at Sixth Form College took four years, at the end of which he had gained eight "O" levels and three "A" levels. Although he was now able to take a different view of his intellectual capability, he continued to experience a sense of academic inferiority, which contributed to his poor self-belief and lack of confidence in social situations.

Subsequently, he became a solicitor and settled in a multicultural part of Bristol with his wife and two children. He became an elder in a large Elim Pentecostal church in the year 2000, and a partner in a large Bristol city legal practice, until a series of events led him to a mid-life career change. Neurological dysfunction in 2003 and subsequent knee surgery forced him to take time off work. He recovered well from both conditions, but in reassessing his situation he realised that he was no longer enjoying work. He resigned his legal partnership, planning to develop a mediation practice and hoping ultimately to set up his own counselling practice. Such a major upheaval had its origins in his past.

For many years, Gary had questioned who he really was. Later, he would discover that something was missing – something which centred around his issues with attachment and rejection. Having been mentored from a distance by Rob Parsons, of Care for the Family, his attempts to understand and deal with his problems led him to gravitate towards relationship issues and counselling. As a Christian interested in counselling, the next logical step was to put the two together. In 1986, Gary became a founding member of the Network Christian Counselling Agency.

During the interim period, he continued to work both as a solicitor and as a mediator. Balancing such a full-on life was tricky and nearly proved impossible after he was deeply pained by his father's death in 1999. Nevertheless, he did not give up, and in 2003 began training to be a counsellor with Relate. He experienced self-discovery. Formal employment commenced with Relate Avon in May 2003, since when Gary has successfully counselled many couples and individuals with relationship issues, working with both heterosexual and homosexual persons.

Annual appraisals confirmed his capabilities in providing full services to Relate clients but he wanted to extend the range of what he could offer. Thus, in 2006, he began to undertake various postgraduate diplomas in counselling. As a result, he became a member of the British Association of Counsellors and Therapists (BACP); the next stage was to become a member of the British Association for Sexual and Relationship Therapy (BASRT) which, in turn, required him to complete the Relate Postgraduate Diploma in Psycho-sexual Therapy (PST). In commencing this diploma, he noted that it would require him to subscribe to the BASRT Code of Ethics and Principles of Good Practice.

As a relationships counsellor, Gary knew the difference between couple counselling – which focuses on improving the relationship between a couple, including helping them end a relationship well – and psycho-sexual therapy, which deals with a couple's intimate sexual disorder. Treatment plans in psycho-sexual therapy last between four and nine months, during which the therapists facilitate and encourage greater satisfaction in the couple's sexual activity in order to improve the relationship.

The Case

Counsellors typically work under supervision in order to discuss issues and facilitate an outside perspective. Gary had one supervisor for couple counselling and a second for psycho-sexual therapy. In November 2005, he raised an issue with his first supervisor after working with a same sex client. His view was that, as a Christian, it might be difficult for him to counsel same sex couples. In doing so, Gary believed that he was acting in line with the Code of Ethics and Equal Opportunities Policy (EOP). With this supervisor's help, he was able to reflect on his position and to continue to counsel same sex couples. One lesbian client (who attended alone) wrote a card of appreciation for his good work. He then subsequently counselled another lesbian couple who had children together. He felt able to counsel because it was about helping people deal with relationship issues.

During this period of his working life as a counsellor, Gary was acutely aware of the questions he was wrestling with, but was determined not to shy away from same sex issues. In facing his concerns about psycho-sexual therapy, he was able to draw on his previous training and work as a solicitor and mediator. Over the years he had worked on negligence cases, sat on medical ethics committees and advised the National Health Service; he thus felt well-placed to deal with his present issues and was pleased that the "safe environment" of supervision had allowed him to address and apparently resolve them to everyone's satisfaction. Indeed, he commented that this was just what five years training with Relate had taught him to do! Moreover, he believed that he and his first supervisor had a personal and professional relationship based on respect.

Towards the end of 2006, Gary began to be supervised by his second (psycho-sexual therapy) supervisor. Concerned right from the start by her headmistress style, he became more assertive but the relationship rapidly deteriorated, mirroring the rejection he was beginning to experience in his own marriage. Furthermore, in commencing the PST course, Gary was unaware that he would have more problems and challenges in this field than appeared to be the case for other therapists. However, the subject did not arise during his supervision sessions until mid-2007, when his supervisor brought up the need to discuss what type of clients could be allocated to him as a trainee. At this stage, there was no mention of any potential difficulties associated with his religious beliefs, and indeed in 2007 his views were still developing concerning counselling same sex couples.

On 22nd July 2007, Gary arrived at Relate to undertake his usual counselling session. Without prior discussion, he was asked if he might discuss his views concerning same sex sexual practices with a key manager at Relate. Gary pointed out that his views had not yet crystallised but did give an outline of what he perceived to be potential conflicts between his faith and the provision of sex therapy to same sex couples. He emphasised that couple counselling *per se* posed no difficulties for him. His manager's response was that Gary might have to deal with same sex couples in sex therapy and asked him to reconsider his position.

Gary then met with his manager and his psycho-sexual therapy supervisor four weeks later. To his considerable surprise, they did not accept his argument that treating the sexual issues that arise in couple counselling is not the same as treating those that come up in psycho-sexual therapy. Their view was that there was no difference, despite clearly stated written information to the contrary. Furthermore, they made it clear that Relate could not identify the nature of any partnerships before cases could be referred to Gary and that screening him from same sex couples would place an increased and disproportionate burden on other counsellors. Gary would also have to share his views with other counsellors when attending courses. In listening to these views of his superiors, Gary was left feeling that a great deal of time and energy were being spent implementing plans of action for a scenario that had not (and might never) occur; equally, if it did, it could easily be managed.

In December 2007, Gary became aware that external support was being offered to him. Aware of circulating rumours, Gary now wondered whether other counsellors had concluded that he was homophobic; there was also a suggestion that a petition had been organised, seeking his dismissal. Gary had always seen himself as approachable and well-liked by colleagues. But it now appeared that seemingly private conversations within supervisions had become public knowledge. He concluded that a number of individuals wished to remove him from his job because of his Christian beliefs.

In that month he attended his usual training weekend in Doncaster. One of the trainers took him aside to inform him that his psycho-sexual therapy supervisor had put a "what if" scenario to her, via the Relate helpline, having identified Gary as holding a particular stance. This helpline exists for counsellors to get guidance and advice and is covered by very senior Relate counsellors and therapists. Gary was naturally deeply concerned that his supervisor had informed "outside" individuals about his religious views, clearly seeking to undermine him. This amounted to both a breach of ethics and of a "duty of care" to a person under supervision. He had not received prior warning of this course of action, nor, in his opinion, was it necessary. What compelling reason was there for the trainer to be aware of this information and why was he specifically identified?

His confidentiality shot, Gary felt obliged to share what was happening in the centre in Bristol, to the concern of the trainer who later sent a written statement endorsing his acceptable ethical practice as a psycho-sexual therapy student, as observed over the previous year. Gary would continue to keep this trainer informed of developments at the centre, including his first reinstatement and subsequent suspension.

Importantly, Gary had still not, at this point, finalised his views concerning sex therapy for same sex couples, merely seeing potential conflict which had not yet arisen. He was aware that all counsellors face personal, moral and ethical issues and that supervision and training was necessary for insight and reflective understanding. He had hoped that his journey within psycho-sexual therapy supervision would enable him to reach a satisfactory outcome, as had taken place within couple counselling. Sadly, this would not take place.

On 12th December 2007, he received a letter from his manager, requesting that by one week hence he must agree to work with same sex couples in both couple counselling and psycho-sexual therapy. Failure to do so might result in disciplinary action. Gary responded by pointing out the self-serving nature of the letter and events progressed rapidly. In early January 2008, Gary contacted Andrea Williams at the Christian Legal Centre, initially for her thoughts on the letter he had received from his manager. This contact would prove not only highly supportive but would have far-reaching implications. The same month, he was also called to an meeting. The result: due to his failure to give relevant assurances that he would work with same sex couples in sex therapy, he was suspended on full pay, pending further investigation.

Four days later, this investigative meeting took place. Gary emphasised that he would continue to comply with the equal opportunities policy and that if any issues arose, he would discuss them in supervision and with management. As a result, he was welcomed back to work. However, on the very day he resumed work, his suspicions concerning a petition was confirmed. Eleven counsellors were signatories to a petition to have him dismissed but, shockingly, not one had ever approached him to discuss their concerns.

His first supervisor then contacted him. He welcomed this chance to re-connect after all the recent difficulties, but during the conversation he discovered that all she wanted was to hear his views first-hand in order to explain them to other counsellors. She also thought he had changed his mind in terms of working with same sex couples and their sex issues. When he explained that he hadn't, the phone call became tense and ended with Gary concerned about a further possible breach of confidentiality and that his personal religious views were being sought for the benefit of a third party.

Later in January 2008, Gary learnt that his psycho-sexual therapy supervisor had resigned and would be replaced by a lady who had herself supervised the outgoing supervisor. He began psycho-sexual therapy supervision with her, which continued until his dismissal.

It took a further nine months for Gary to learn of this new supervisor's role in his dismissal. In hindsight, it made her appointment as his supervisor all the more distasteful. Back in February 2008, he had received an email from his manager, including an attachment which contained a summary of the private and confidential issues discussed over three to four years of supervisions with his first supervisor. Again, this amounted to a huge breach of confidentiality and duty of care to him.

Effectively, she had acted not as a supportive supervisor but as an interrogator with ulterior motives, who then switched seamlessly to becoming an informant. He had never, anywhere, come across such unprofessional behaviour. Not being a member of BACP herself, she was not accountable to any professional body for her actions, a situation Gary deemed utterly unacceptable and certainly not in the public interest.

For there was no exceptional reason which allowed for disclosure of this confidential information. Such disclosure not only seriously undermined the counsellor/supervisor relationship but also fell foul of the BACP Code. In short, the supervisor felt that his religious views prevented him from working with Relate and that she had lost faith in his ability, a view which Gary considered an abuse of her position.

In February 2008, Gary was asked for his comments on her statement. He reiterated his position, namely that he would work with same sex couples and would continue to discuss any problems with his supervisor and manager. He added, however, that seeking to exercise religious rights and freedoms in the workplace did not amount to discrimination against others. Four days later, he attended a disciplinary hearing at which his psycho-sexual therapy supervisor's summary document was used as evidence, Charges of gross misconduct were presented on the basis that he had never shown any intention of complying with Relate's ethics policy in working with same sex couples and same sex issues. During the disciplinary process his clients would be reallocated.

With his confidentiality breached, and misrepresented as a homophobe, Gary was then dismissed on 18th March 2008 for gross misconduct, without notice and without payment in lieu. Not only did this dismissal clearly sever his working position in Relate, it tarnished his previously unblemished career and position in relation to the church and the Law Society, as well as in the sphere of counselling.

Ten days later Gary lodged a complaint with the BACP. Oddly, not only was his first supervisor not a member of this organisation, but neither was Relate Avon. By contrast, Relate Doncaster had membership. Thus, although Relate Avon worked in accordance with BACP's ethical framework, not being a member meant that the organisation itself was not accountable and thus could not be investigated.

In May 2008, Gary's dismissal was upheld. Professionally, the implications of Relate's actions have been severe. The failure of the BACP to investigate his complaint against his supervisor and Relate was painful enough, but Gary has subsequently found it very difficult to get supervision for his evolving sex therapy practice. Unable also to gain PST clients has delayed the completion of his coursework and, his psycho-sexual therapy Diploma remained in limbo.

Seeking to advertise his counselling services to build up a private practice has proved unsuccessful and other doors also closed. Invited to lead a sex therapy course for trainee GPs in his area, he accepted, only for the offer to be withdrawn. Furthermore, another key professional body – COSRT (College of Sex and Relationship Therapists) have refused him membership but declined to supply a reason why. This affects his ability to practise as a sex therapist. On the plus side, however, he did complete the Diploma in Couple Counselling and became a full member of the BACP.

Looking back, Gary reflected that he had always acted professionally as a counsellor and never refused to work with a client. Though singled out by a group of people for his Christian faith, he still believes that he could re-establish positive working relationships with colleagues and would like to return to working with Relate. Such a substantial organisation, staffed with individuals from different backgrounds and faiths should have been able to accommodate him. At the very least, his couple counselling should have been allowed to continue whilst the issue of psycho-sexual therapy remained under review.

His dismissal has not only restricted what he had hoped would be a successful career change but has had a major financial impact on Gary. Having formerly been a legal partner in a large firm, he was now on benefits. Snubbed even by the Christian counselling agency of which he was a founder member, the pain he felt on separating from his wife in 2006 was even more severe than that felt when his father had died, seven years previously. With other family members severely ill, and even his church friends taking sides, all seemed lost. Giving up on life, he asked his Father to take him home. Feeling that a motor accident would do the job, his wish appeared to come true when a tyre blew at speed on a motorway. Instead, God spared him. Gary would discover why, over the course of the next three years.

In 2007, Gary realised that he needed some healing. Reluctantly entering therapy himself, he cried until there were no more tears. Over the next year, he worked in London, living in the same house as his wife whilst awaiting their divorce. Life remained full-on but the pain and financial pressures remained severe. In the midst of the maelstrom, he needed hope – and God provided.

There, in the midst of the trauma, God gave him a vision of the future and re-affirmed a prophecy given some twenty-five years earlier. Now he knew what to do and where God was taking him. In essence, he had been given the responsibility to teach and counsel, helping others to move from conflict to freedom, allowing them to reach their full potential. The effect of this revelation on Gary personally was equally momentous. In reaching a place where he was so much closer to God, he could truly say that he would go through all the pain again to get to this level of walk with Him. No longer living a "B" life as a Christian, Gary's awareness of the reality of God became greater than before.

Spiritually charged, Gary found that that his personality profile changed. A life-long introvert, he had now become more bold, willing to stand up and speak. And God had another gift for him.

In 2007, over a year into his separation, he attended a prayer meeting in which he asked for his marriage to be restored, hoping to win back the wife he still loved desperately. A young woman sat next to him. Unable subsequently to explain what exactly happened, something went out from him. Many months later, the Father spoke and offered him a choice. Gary admitted his feelings towards the young lady, but remained adamant that he wanted his wife back. To this end, he had kept clear boundaries in terms of never being with women alone unless – or until – he became divorced. Tearfully, he reminded the Father that he hated divorce and that he had chosen his wife and that was final and that he did not want this conversation again!

Nevertheless, divorce did take place, just when the Relate cases were in full flow in 2008. Gary moved out of the family home a few weeks later. Very shortly afterwards, the Father gave him a gift which, at first, he could not fully accept, considering it not right. All counsellors know that it takes at least two years to come to terms with divorce; how would people react to this new lady coming into his life so quickly? Reminded of Psalm 23:5, a table prepared in the presence of his enemies, Gary still felt the time was not right to eat. It took a minister to help him recognise how he was treating God's gift. Further affirmation was given at a conference in London, and the Father began to show him how the abundance spoken about in John 10:10 was being rebuilt in his life, and how it should underpin his therapeutic practice. God had over-ridden his choice to have his wife back. Later, He was kind enough to tell Gary why: the pain he had suffered was for a bigger purpose which would continue to be revealed to him over time.

Over the next two years, Gary grew to love the gift he had been given. Even his children were drawn towards his new lady, and in July 2010 the couple married. With his new vision and purpose, Gary's life is being rebuilt, totally dependent on God. With plans under way for a seven-bedroom house for marriage and relationship rebuilding, his aim to refresh couples and singles enters a new phase. With the future bright, Gary could have chosen to close the book on the injustice he had suffered. But the devastation it had caused, allied to the principle of fighting for the right of Christians to practise their faith at work, led him to agree to the CLC taking his case further.

Following his dismissal in March 2008 for gross

misconduct, an appeal took place in April which was rejected. The next step was an Employment Tribunal, claiming discrimination and unfair and wrongful dismissal, but the judgment in January 2009 found against him. An Employment Appeal Tribunal in November 2009 equally rejected Gary's arguments, ruling that the Tribunal had been correct to dismiss his claims. Not one to give up lightly, Mr Diamond went to the Court of Appeal. His first request was turned down in January 2010, but his second request came before Lord Justice Laws. After examining the application, he was sufficiently impressed with the reach of the arguments concerning religious rights, and the supporting witness statement from Lord Carey, the former Archbishop of Canterbury, to look further into the matter. However, having done so, in April 2010 he still dismissed the application!

Having exhausted all legal avenues in the UK, five months later, on 29th September 2010, Mr Diamond applied to the European Court of Human Rights in Strasbourg. Two years later, in September 2012, the case was eventually heard, along with three other UK Christian cases, including that of Shirley Chaplin (Chapter One). The eagerly-awaited judgment was revealed three months later, in January 2013. In it, the Court accepted that Mr McFarlane's refusal to counsel homosexual couples was motivated by – and a manifestation of – his orthodox Christian beliefs concerning marriage and sexual relationships and that the State, under Article 9, was obliged to secure these rights. But the Court had to assess whether a fair balance was struck between the competing interests of the individual and the community as a whole. In making this assessment, the Court was aware that the loss of his job was a severe sanction with grave consequences, but on the other hand Gary had voluntarily begun training in psycho-sexual counselling, knowing that

Relate's Equal Opportunities Policy meant that filtering of clients would not be possible.

Weighing it up, the Court decided that the most important factor was that the employer acted to implement its policy of providing a service without discrimination, and that in doing so, the wide margin of appreciation which benefits State authorities in deciding where to strike the balance between competing rights had not been exceeded, and thus the refusal by domestic courts to uphold Mr McFarlane's complaints had not violated Article 9. The case was dismissed. The court had recognised his legal right but had abdicated its role in ensuring such a right by invoking the "margin of appreciation" test.

But this is not the end of the matter. Persistence remains the key, for Gary's case, along with that of Shirley Chaplin (see Chapter One), has not only attracted huge media interest but has been the subject of many journals and much teaching. Seen as definitive cases for religious freedom in the UK and the rest of Europe in terms of manifestation of faith and human rights, one last card remained to be played. In April 2013, Mr Diamond applied for both to be referred to the Grand Chamber of the European Court of Human Rights. Sadly, permission was not granted but, as with Chaplin, much has been gained along the way which should be of benefit to future cases going through UK courts.

7

Lesley Pilkington
The Reparative Therapist

Lesley Pilkington grew up in Australia, a country she loved.
Several of her ancestors had played prominent roles in the
early life of the colony – her grandmother was the first
female barrister in Queensland, but could not practise, owing
to her father's views on young ladies working for a living.
She and her sisters instead campaigned for women's rights
in those early years of Australia's history. These and other
family members motivated Lesley to make a difference for
the common good.

Marriage to an Englishman led to their two children
having dual nationality after the family moved to the UK.
The move did not just benefit the youngsters, it allowed
Lesley to gain a singular perspective on life. As far back
as she could remember, she had thought deeply and felt
anguish about the meaning of life. Coming from a family of
non-believers, at the age of twenty-nine she experienced a
dramatic, audible encounter with God, had a vision, and was
filled with the Holy Spirit. Working at that time in a London
psychiatric hospital, she was too terrified to tell anyone of
her audible "voice" in case she, too, was sectioned under
the Mental Health Act!

As time went by, she felt totally different and knew
that her life had changed. A deep ache and void had been
replaced by a sense of fullness and peace. She had more

compassion and concern for people. Asking a churchgoing neighbour if he knew of a church where she could find God proved to have been inspired – they attended together and this proved to be the beginning of her walk with God. The journey has been blessed as she developed her life's calling, safe in the knowledge that He would never let her go; it has also proved difficult and costly, not least over the past three years, following an encounter at a conference which changed her life.

For over twenty years, Lesley has been a psychotherapist and Christian counsellor, working in doctors' surgeries as well as in a small private practice. Beyond work, her faith has led her into prayer ministry and prophecy in the local church, as well as to preach in Africa. As a Christian counsellor, Lesley has been privileged to deal with issues like anxiety and depression, identity crises and sexual confusion, along with grief, loss, trauma and self-harm. Reducing anguish in the general public has kept her very busy, and her role has been recognised through membership of six professional bodies, including the British Association for Counselling and Psychotherapy (BACP).

The Case

In April 2009, Lesley attended a two-day conference in London organised by the National Association of Research and Therapy into Homosexuality (NARTH), Anglican Mainstream and CARE. It was thus both a secular conference with Judaeo-Christian values and mainstream Christian. The title of the conference was: Sex and the City: Redeeming Sex Today. Described as ideal for clergy, rabbis, psychologists, therapists, educators and others concerned about the plethora of sexual issues confronting us today, its topics included same sex attraction (discussing the possibility of change), mentoring the sexually broken, pornography, marriage and how the Bible deals with the family and sexual issues.

Owing to previous aggression by the gay community who disapproved of academic enquiry and free speech in these matters, there was a vetting procedure for entrance to the conference. Most of the people present, although not all, were Christians, and each day began and ended with prayer. Lesley herself attended in a private capacity, but also as the parent of a son in a homosexual lifestyle. Her aim was to meet with colleagues and other parents with a similar background to discuss personal stories.

During a break in the conference, Lesley was approached by a man in his early thirties, who referred to himself as "Matthew Stins". He told her that he was looking for a therapist for "treatment for his same sex attraction" as he was unhappy with his gay lifestyle, now meaningless to him. He desired change, and having initially approached another psychotherapist, who was at the conference but lived in Northern Ireland, he preferred a therapist who was nearer London. Whilst such self-referral was unusual, Lesley believed him. Unaware that, in reality, "Matthew" was an investigative journalist providing false information, who had gained entrance to the conference using equally fictitious details, Lesley chatted informally with him. Learning that he had been brought up as a Christian, she asked him to explain a bit more about himself and whether he understood biblical values. In turn she disclosed that she was an accredited counsellor with the BACP but only worked on same sex attraction issues as a biblical Christian counsellor, using "Reparative Therapy" with the "change is possible" agenda, as was discussed at the conference.

She went on to state that any literature suggested would be Christian and that she intended to work with the Holy

Spirit. Matthew replied that he understood this language, owing to his Roman Catholic background. Lesley added that she personally provided no other options on the area of same sex attraction, and that if he sought a different approach, she would happily refer him on. She requested that he consider what had been discussed before deciding whether it felt right for him. Later in the conference, he approached her again. Comfortable with what she had suggested, he wished to proceed. He said that they "were on the same wavelength". It would later be clear that he had no intention of switching to another way of working as he wanted to "expose" this particular model, with a BACP member as his victim. Lesley gave Matthew her card and asked him to ring her to make an appointment for an initial assessment session, during which she would explain more about the therapy.

On 6th May 2009, Matthew emailed Lesley, arranging to meet. Before doing so, he asked whether any preparation, including Bible extracts, might benefit him. Lesley replied that he should simply attend, for her practice involved prayer and working with the Holy Spirit.

The assessment took place in Lesley's home later that month. During this session, Lesley felt led to pray more than usual, and the meeting lasted longer than the hour set aside which, she had explained in advance, was not unusual for an initial assessment. "Matthew", in turn, asked many questions, which Lesley assumed meant he was exploring whether this was right for him. She would later discover to the contrary that all points raised were targeted to his undercover investigations which he later wrote about in national newspapers. To do so, he recorded the sessions without Lesley's prior knowledge or permission, with transcripts being produced. At the end of this first session, "Matthew" said he was "on the right path" and asked for several follow-up meetings. A second session was therefore planned, this time via Skype as Lesley's life was at that time split between the UK and Norway where her husband was working.

All appeared well, until a further session in the UK failed to take place after Matthew suffered "some kind of seizure". He then failed to attend a re-scheduled appointment in June 2009. The reason became clear when he telephoned Lesley to reveal his true nature. Having led her to believe that his name was "Matthew", in truth he was Patrick Strudwick, a journalist with the gay newspaper, "Pink News." Admitting to having given false information about himself, his motive was not therapy but to expose her and people like her. He admitted to having secretly taped all their discussions and sessions and even the conference itself, despite having signed an agreement not to bring recording equipment into the conference. He now intended to make a complaint to her professional body, the BACP, in order that she would lose her job; furthermore, as a journalist, he would write about her in national newspapers in order to discredit her work with those who were unhappy with their same sex attraction.

Although Lesley does not frighten easily, the aggressive and intimidating nature of Patrick's threats shook her. Struggling to take in what was happening, she felt betrayed and angry as well as fearful. Eventually, she recovered enough to tell him that she would seek legal advice of her own in response to his threats. She also called the police, feeling that she and her family might require some protection.

Most of what Patrick threatened took place. He contacted the surgery where she worked and wrote about her in national newspapers. These articles proved to be manipulative and complete distortions of the therapeutic relationship between them. They also violated all confidentiality between themselves as "Christians" – itself, of course, another lie. His aim was to ridicule, mock, bully and intimidate. Notably, he had also "exposed" the psychiatrist from Northern Ireland, whom he had met at the same conference – a double betrayal.

Seven months later, in January 2010, the BACP received a letter from Patrick, alleging that Lesley had "acted unprofessionally and breached the Ethical Framework for Good Practice in Counselling and Psychotherapy ... and contravened the Code of Ethics and Practice for Counsellors 1998." The broad sweep of his anger centred on the very thing he had asked for in therapy, namely the possibility of change. Opposing this concept, he believed that homosexuals could not change and should not be given the opportunity to do so.

At no stage did Patrick attempt to contact Lesley or provide written explanation to resolve the matter (in accordance with the above Ethical Framework). In a subsequent letter to the BACP he merely stated that "the nature of the complaint is so severe that [contacting the respondent] would be futile." The Pre-Hearing Assessment Panel considered his complaint and decided that there was a case to answer.

The BACP wrote to Lesley on 29th June 2010, stating that the complaint received alleged contravention of the minimum standard of good practice as outlined in the Ethical Framework.

In particular –

- Lesley had prayed to God to heal the complainant of his homosexuality;
- Lesley had an agenda that homosexuality was wrong and that gay people can change;
- Lesley attempted to inflict these views on Patrick;
- Lesley failed to provide good quality of care. Clear boundaries were absent, resulting in poor timekeeping, making personal disclosures about her son and introducing Patrick to her husband;
- Lesley disclosed personal views on lifestyle and sexual

orientation which were prejudiced and disrespectful of his lifestyle;

- Lesley failed to adequately explore all the available options, choosing to lead him down one particular route of therapy, thus contravening the ethical principles of Autonomy and Beneficence.

In response, Lesley wrote back to the BACP in July 2010, explaining the background to her counselling sessions with Mr Strudwick. Taking Patrick's allegations in turn, she admitted to praying at the beginning and end of the first session, as explained to Patrick previously, but did not ask God to heal him of his homosexuality, a point confirmed by the transcripts. Furthermore, they had initially agreed to work together within a Christian model. The Bible clearly states that all forms of sexual conduct outside marriage (between one man and one woman) are wrong, with the practice of homosexuality specifically condemned in several Old Testament and New Testament passages. Denying having an agenda, she did believe that gay people can change, a view supported by 1 Corinthians 6:9–11, which states that change is possible. Again, the Ethical Framework was in no way contravened.

With regard to the third point, he had come to her repeatedly expressing the view that he was unhappy with his homosexual lifestyle and wanted "treatment for same sex attraction". This was crucial, as Lesley only worked in the area of same sex attraction with those wishing to change, a point she had made clear to Patrick before any therapy began and contradicting Patrick's statement that she had attempted to inflict her views on him.

Lesley agreed with the allegation that her timekeeping had not been "perfect" but was unclear how spending ninety minutes (rather than the allocated one hour) in the initial session constituted a breach of the Ethical Framework. Prayer had taken a little time, as had allowing him time to ask as many questions as he had desired. In her twenty year experience, an hour and a quarter spent in these initial assessments achieved the best results. With respect to her son, Patrick himself first brought this subject up and indeed admitted to the BACP that he had gained this knowledge prior to the sessions from the conference; even if he hadn't, disclosure of personal information is validated by "The Theory and Practice of Counselling 2005".

In struggling to understand which part of the Ethical Framework she had contravened, Lesley turned her attention to his complaint concerning her husband. Halfway through the first session, Patrick asked to use the bathroom. In so doing, he coincidentally met her husband, who was coming down the stairs. Lesley introduced the two men and was pleased that this client (like other male clients) was aware that for security purposes she was not alone in the house. From study of the transcripts, it appears that Patrick used the bathroom to change the recording tape around. It is therefore likely that the two men met only through this technical requirement and that this complaint was simply a smokescreen.

The allegations concerning Lesley's perceived prejudicial and disrespectful views on his homosexual orientation and lifestyle were presumably linked to a section within the Ethical Framework, entitled "Keeping Trust," which disallows any personal views of practitioners from prejudicing the professional relationship with clients. However, Lesley's personal views were entirely clear *de novo*, with Christian boundaries being established. Denying prejudice, Lesley instead contended that the relationship was guided by her professional views on sexual orientation. Patrick's statement early in counselling that it was "useful" when someone was "very honest" with him, would also seem to have contradicted any sense of disrespect.

Finally, the Principles of Autonomy and Beneficence imply the client's right to be self-governing and the commitment to promoting the client's well-being. Lesley had given accurate information in advance of services being offered and regularly sought his consent with no attempt to manipulate him against his will; indeed, his clearly expressed will was to "change". The purpose of the counselling sessions was not to explore all available options but to pursue the one agreed, namely "treatment for same sex attraction". Had Lesley acted differently, she would have breached his autonomy as well as that section of the Ethical Framework which states that "over-riding a client's wishes or consent is a serious matter that requires adequate and reasoned justification." Patrick's "known wishes" were clear and she had acted wholly in accordance with those wishes. This completed her response to the BACP.

By now the CLC had become involved and issued a press release about her story. The hearing was set for January 2011 but adjourned, partly because Lesley intended to report to the police that a professional witness, Dr Byrd, had been intimidated after receiving "negative and discomforting communication" from UK and US activists. The police later chose to regard this as a "hate related incident".

The Professional Conduct Panel met in May 2011 to consider the complaint. Paul Diamond of the CLC represented Mrs Pilkington. The panel was aware that the complainant was an undercover journalist who claimed to be a Christian and specifically requested treatment from her for same sex attraction. They were also informed that she was unaware that he had audio-recorded the sessions.

Despite these obvious deceptions, the panel upheld almost all the complaints made by Patrick Strudwick against Lesley. Her poor time-keeping in the first session was criticised as being disconcerting to the complainant, and the personal disclosures concerning her son's rugby-playing reflected her attitude towards Patrick's masculinity. Introducing him to her husband without prior warning was seen as thoughtless, as was sharing her opinion that same sex attraction had similarities with depression and that it is addictive behaviourally, like alcoholism. The panel also commented on her exploring the family dynamics including any possible bullying or sexual abuse and whether there was any freemasonry within the family.

Furthermore, the panel commented on her advice to keep some distance from his homosexual friends and concerning his body posture and eye contact, which were linked to confidence. Their opinion was that Mrs Pilkington had been disrespectful in the dogmatic way in which she had presented her views and that her diagnoses, given so early in treatment, were premature and reckless with no evidence of empathy or that she had listened attentively to the complexity of Mr. Strudwick's experiences.

It was conceded, however, that Mr Strudwick had not expected Lesley to explore all the therapeutic options available, and that he had agreed to work with her with the goal of changing his sexuality using a biblical approach.

The panel also decided that Mrs Pilkington had allowed her preconceived views about gay lifestyle and sexual orientation to affect her relationship with Mr Strudwick prejudicially. The panel members were also not satisfied that she had kept up to date with the latest knowledge and research about the development of human sexuality, focusing only on training that confirmed her own beliefs.

The panel then looked at Lesley's argument that Mr Strudwick could not be deemed a client (and thus not subject to redress) as, in actuality, he was an undercover journalist. A therapeutic relationship had therefore never existed. Rejecting this argument, the members concluded that he did fall within the definition of a "client" receiving counselling services from a practitioner. The panel also discarded her claim that he had derived some benefit from the sessions.

Accordingly, the panel was unanimous in its decision that these findings amounted to professional malpractice. The panel judged that Mrs Pilkington had failed to provide the complainant with adequate professional services that could reasonably be expected of a practitioner exercising reasonable care and skill. In mitigation, the panel acknowledged that Mr Strudwick had misled her, not least in saying "Amen" at the end of prayers, and that he had "become more religious again recently", lulling her into a false sense of security. He had also considerably manipulated the content of the sessions to meet his own agenda.

The sanction applied was severe. Mrs Pilkington's BACP Accredited status lapsed with immediate effect. Within a month, she was compelled to submit written reflections on her learning and understanding of the issues raised in the complaint, and by the end of a year had to provide further written submissions indicating the changes in her practice, not least in boundary management. She would also have to attend courses to learn of different ways of working in the field of same sex attraction and provide reports from supervisors on ethical working with all her clients. Only then could she apply for reinstatement of her accreditation.

Having lost the initial hearing in May, Lesley sought leave to appeal. The BACP were obliged to place the case before an independent appeals solicitor, who found for Lesley, ruling that a fair trial had not taken place as the BACP had not looked at all the evidence. Specifically, the association had ignored the two tape recorded conversations; had they been heard, the outcome might have been very different. An appeal hearing was therefore granted. In the meantime, Lord Carey, along with other senior figures, wrote in support of her case, stating that she should still be able to provide therapy. However, following the appeal in May 2012, the BACP were adamant that she lost her senior accredited status, despite being fully cognisant of the deceit and trickery employed by the gay undercover journalist.

Perhaps the most extraordinary aspect of this case is that Mrs Pilkington has nothing to hide. There has never been any secret about "change is possible" therapy or, indeed, concerning biblical counselling. At any time, "Matthew" could have openly interviewed her about her work. Undercover journalism was quite unnecessary, indeed absurd. Instead, he pursued a year-long, vicious campaign against her, for his own agenda.

Very destructive though this has proved, of equal concern is the BACP's attitude towards different models of treatment. Clearly antithetical to the biblical model, Lesley wonders whether the only acceptable stance for their practitioners is to be "gay-affirming". If so, the considerable pressure from certain members of the gay community to suppress academic enquiry, free speech and methods of treatment which they disapprove of, has proved successful. Lies have been held to be the truth, as such political correctness has nothing to do with reason, understanding or knowledge. Challenging such an ethos is nothing less than a fight for freedom – not only freedom for therapists and Christian counsellors to do their work, but also for those in a homosexual lifestyle, with all its inherent dangers, who desire to change.

Lesley's concern that BACP policy is purely gay-affirming has been proven correct. In September 2012, they issued a statement of ethical practice, confirming that, "The BACP opposes any psychological treatment such as reparative or conversion therapy which is based upon the assumption that homosexuality is a mental disorder, or based upon the premise that the client/patient should change his/her sexuality."

The organisation went on to state that the BACP recognises ... that practices such as conversion or reparative therapies have "no medical indication and represent a severe threat to the health and human rights of the affected persons."

Instead, "The BACP believes that socially inclusive, non-judgemental attitudes to people who identify across the diverse range of human sexualities will have positive consequences for those individuals, as well as for the wider society in which they live. There is no rational or ethical reason to treat people who identify within a range of sexualities any differently from those who identify solely as heterosexual."

Over the last three years, Lesley's life has been much affected. Previously, she was just one of many psycho-therapists and Christian counsellors working in the field of same sex attraction. The attentions of the homosexual journalist changed everything. With an explicit agenda – to investigate and expose her and others working in this area – he has caused her much anguish through publishing articles which were both mocking and manipulative. Aiming to close down any support for those wanting to change their homosexual lifestyle has had some success – therapists are now understandably very cautious in tackling this problem; indeed, many no longer work in this area.

With the media in the main supporting the journalist's view, and the BACP still wary of her professionally, Lesley's ability to see clients has suffered. So why does she regard what has happened to her not only as stressful, but as hugely exhilarating? Why is she, unlike others who have deserted the cause, still passionate about helping people troubled in this area? In short, what has enabled this "ordinary person with an ordinary life" not just to persevere but to thrive in extreme adversity? The answer lies, I think, in her willingness to adapt and change, whilst holding on to the essentials in life.

Prior to these events taking place, Lesley had already struggled with the homosexuality of her beloved son. When faced with this new trial in the public arena, she was able to lean on the support structures – her family and friends – which were already in place in her private life. Moreover, having always kept her focus on the Lord throughout the ups and downs of life, she knew that He does most definitely take on our burdens. If this was liberating, more releasing was the knowledge that her previous "good" reputation had gone. No longer had she to strive for something which ultimately matters little.

Free indeed, Lesley is now totally against the same sex "marriage" agenda. With delicious irony, her small-scale campaigning in opposition to the homosexual agenda includes speaking at conferences! She had never thought her life would develop this way, but her passion for helping the needy has meant that she must speak the truth. Naturally, this involves her affirming that real help and change is only through the death and resurrection of Jesus Christ, words that she will continue to bring to our corrupt, hurting and lost generation while God gives her life on this earth. Through her "exposure", God has enabled her to preach the gospel quite extensively, particularly into the Asian community, via BBC Asia Radio.

In 2012, having made her jump through hoops of extra training and supervision, the BACP discovered that their pressure on Lesley to become gay-affirming had not succeeded as her work had not changed. Deciding not to re-accredit her, their recognition was no longer needed when Lesley was made aware of a new body of counsellors. Applying to join the Association of Christian Counsellors (ACC) in the summer of 2012, she was accepted, and now practises her trade in freedom and without fear.

The Lord is opening new doors, as she plans over the coming year to enter the public sphere again by doing a video with her clients, explaining how to move away from SSA (same-sex attraction) to heterosexuality. And if there was ever any doubt in her motivation to speak, one illustration dispels it forever. Some homosexual activists have a slogan and banner which they bring to demonstrations proclaiming, "love has no name". How sad, how lost without hope. Lesley would say to them, "Love DOES have a name and it is Jesus. Allow me to introduce you."

PART FOUR

SHARING FAITH AT WORK

8

Wayne Follett
The Teacher

Wayne has been employed by a County Council since December 2001 as a supply teacher for children unable to attend school through illness or other physical conditions.

The Case

In April 2008, Wayne drove to a student's home for a lesson. Previously, he had a good relationship with the family and was greeted by the mother who offered him a cup of tea. The mother asked the child to come downstairs, but she was not very well so the two adults spent time talking about the books that they were currently reading, whilst waiting for her to appear.

When the pupil came downstairs, it was evident that she was too ill to take part in the lesson. When specifically asked by Wayne whether she wanted to be taught, she declined. At this point, Wayne was so concerned by the pupil's condition that he continued to talk to the mother and child, wanting to encourage the family. So he related to them how his faith in God had helped him in difficult situations. In particular, he described how God had miraculously saved him from being killed by a tractor running out of control down a slope, when he was sixteen. He went on to say that children, when they die, go to heaven, and that there were people praying for the family. Following this up with a request to pray for them, he noted that the child looked at the mother, who informed him that their family did not believe. Clearly understanding that this statement meant that they had declined his offer, Wayne did not pray. Instead, he asked whether the mother wished him to cancel the next lesson. Learning that she did not, he left the house shortly afterwards.

Returning to base, Wayne downloaded lesson plans for various students, spoke to a colleague and taught another student. Following this, he received a message that the Head of the (Education) Centre wished to see him urgently. Aware that this particular lady only saw people without a set appointment if there was a major problem, he was naturally concerned. He then learnt that his immediate boss had been to see the family with whom he had spent part of the morning. He went to see her and was told that she did not wish to discuss the matter then, but the implication was that he had done something very wrong that morning. This came as a shock, for he had never suspected on leaving the house that any offence had taken place. Asking whether he would be sacked, he was informed that certainly he would not be teaching that afternoon. His boss would cover his lessons and, until further notice, it was suggested that he should go for a coffee or drive home and await a phone call.

Aware that the mother must have made a complaint against him, and feeling very awkward, Wayne drove to a Tesco car park. Whilst there, he rang a few friends, asking for prayer, and then contacted the Centre; his superiors would see him that afternoon.

Whilst waiting, he read Psalm 23 and then entered the room, still clutching his Bible. His boss took the lead, asking him whether he would like to present his own version of events or simply hear what the mother had to say. Trembling, and struggling to put two words together, he chose the latter.

Firstly, and to his considerable surprise, Wayne learnt that the parent had previously complained about him, following an earlier visit to the home. It was not clear why these parental concerns had been hidden from him, nor did he understand why the mother claimed that he had "demanded" a cup of tea. Returning to the present day, the mother alleged that both she and the child had been distressed by Wayne relating his testimony and by offering prayer to them. The mother went on to say that Wayne had "imposed" his religion on them and that this was the second time that this had happened. The upshot was that they did not wish him to tutor in their home ever again.

Very annoyed, Wayne's boss asked why he had not followed her previous advice concerning matters of faith. In truth, not only had he not been made aware of the mother's feelings, he had never received any written instruction not to pray or speak about his faith – merely verbal counselling not to do so. Nevertheless, it was considered that he had stepped beyond his professional duties by crossing a boundary. In future, he should simply not talk about his faith, especially in a minor's home where such an approach might be deemed to constitute bullying.

By now, seeing his intention to kindly encourage the family become twisted to give a totally different impression, Wayne could barely answer any questions. Instead, all he could do was relate, once again, that he was alive today because God had miraculously saved his life.

In conclusion, his boss agreed that Wayne had been an exemplary teacher, but his services would no longer be required. Wayne took this to mean that he had been dismissed on the spot. Asking what would have happened if he had been a contracted member of staff, his superiors retorted that the matter would have been more thoroughly investigated and he would have ended up in a worse position. When asked whether he had anything to add, he replied, "Yes – if you are ever in a difficult position, pray, because God answers prayer."

Sacked for sharing his testimony and for offering prayer, Wayne felt that his dismissal was wrong and unfair. Furthermore, he had been dismissed on the spot, without notice and without investigation having taken place. In his eyes, this amounted to discrimination. The media were alerted, and after they showed interest in his story, the manager contacted Wayne to arrange a meeting.

At the meeting the Head of the Centre began by stating that the Tuition Service had been contacted by one of the child's parents, via a key worker, to ask that all tutors be given a message that the family did not wish to discuss faith matters. The Head acknowledged that Wayne had not attended the particular tuition meeting at which this knowledge was shared and thus had not been made aware of this crucial piece of information. Equally encouragingly, he put forward the management view that it can be appropriate for teachers and tutors to share their faith with a pupil or family, but that professionals need to judge carefully whether this would be acceptable to the person or family concerned. He noted that Wayne had agreed to respect both the wishes of individual families and the guidance from his manager concerning faith issues. He also accepted that there were some procedural and communication issues with supply teachers that needed improvement.

The Head went on to congratulate Wayne for his highly regarded teaching, which had led to "wonderful GCSE outcomes for some pupils". Aware that he had been suspended from further supply work till this meeting, he confirmed that the organisation would not only offer him work in the future, but would make up the hours lost through additional work, or pay him the equivalent.

The meeting had been constructive, but whilst it provided some good news, Wayne remained apprehensive and wanted confirmation in writing as, having been let down by those in authority in the past, he was concerned that the Council's action would not occur. As a result, he felt the matter would best be referred to a tribunal. His fears were then realised when the letter from the Head duly arrived.

Prior to the tribunal, the Council had rather changed its tune. Noting that supply teachers were engaged as self-employed workers, not employees, they were therefore under no obligation to provide work. With no obligation either for Wayne to accept any work offered, there was therefore no employment relationship between the two parties, so the Council denied that Wayne had ever been an employee and was therefore surprised that a claim for "dismissal" had been lodged. Such a claim should be struck out on the grounds that the tribunal did not have the jurisdiction to hear it, and even if it should find that Wayne had been unlawfully dismissed, the Council would submit that any compensation would be inequitable, as Wayne, in their view, had wholly contributed to his dismissal through culpable conduct. Having paid him fully for work done, the Council had no intention to pay for any potential work lost through his suspension.

More positively, however, it was noted that Wayne had agreed to meet the Council to discuss a "goodwill" payment; he was also aware that he could contact their website, should he be interested in further temporary or permanent work with their organisation. In the end the tribunal proved not to be necessary as, with the help of the CLC, the case was settled.

Wayne worked for a private school for six months. In this establishment he was able to offer to pray for students who were learning various subjects. The students were able to excel in their education, helped by the Christian values and prayers which were the foundation stones in this particular school. Such a faith-based system was an eye opener for Wayne. In comparison, so few children in the state system receive the Christian values that used to exist in its curricula. Is it any wonder that riots occur in our cities and towns?

Sadly, due to the recession, several students left the school which caused the employer to offer teachers voluntary redundancy. Wayne left as he was the last employee recruited and felt that he should give others the benefit of remaining in employment.

Subsequently, Wayne became a job seeker for a period of six months. Trying desperately to find employment in this time, he received a few hours' work from the Council. He regarded this as a tremendous miracle as it demonstrated that the Council were prepared to move forward positively.

He then accepted a short-term contract to work for an agency. God had come through for him once again. As one door closes, another is opened by God, through the power of prayer.

Initially, Wayne did not want this account to be published in a book. However, as he prayed about the matter and did his daily reading, he was led by God to make known the power of prayer. God uses prayers – working miracles and changing lives for the better.

Before his dismissal, Wayne had prayed that he would have an opportunity to witness to his boss. Two months earlier, God gave him a dream in which he was in a small office with his bosses, and had felt unhappy. At the time, he believed that it was a bad dream, perhaps due to being tired or eating food that had upset him. Instead, God was warning him of what he would have to go through. The room would prove to be the same, but the shock was greater. Thankfully, God spared him the details of the pain he would encounter.

Note

Names and dates have been changed and the Council not
identified, in order to protect the identity of the teacher
involved.

9

Richard Scott
The GP

Born in 1960 in a middle class area of Cheshire, my childhood was interrupted – and nearly ended – two years later,
when my appendix perforated. Recovering, I was able to
develop a friendship with my neighbour, Richard Bolchover,
who was born just after me. He would introduce me to the
local Jewish community. Sent to Sunday School by atheist
parents until I begged to leave at the age of five, I was
intrigued by the weekly ritual and spiritual purpose which
Richard's family demonstrated and which mine so clearly
lacked. Here was a tiny window into a faith community – the
start of my journey into Christianity.

In 1966, my father obtained a management job in Turkey.
Our year spent there was notable for boys clearly older
than me (but my size) selling bread and shining my shoes.
I had come across poverty for the first time. Far from home
and bombarded by new impressions, I was perhaps now
more open to receive from God. My mother, to her eternal
credit, brought me one book from England: *The Illustrated
Children's Bible*. As she read, the stories captured my
imagination, and a seed was sown that developed years
later, after the family move to Surrey led to my attending
Kingston Grammar School. Famous for its hockey, a game I
grew to love, more importantly the school ran a burgeoning

Christian Union, and its summer camps attracted up to a hundred pupils. Attending CU camp for the third time at the age of fourteen, I responded to a call to give my life to Christ.

All was well whilst at school; problems began at university. Allowing the busyness of student life to relegate God to the periphery, my time in London and Cambridge gave me a hockey blue and a medical degree but no sound footing from which to face adult working life. At the age of twenty-six, things came to a head at Papworth Hospital. A combination of immensely hard work and bad social decisions led my life to finally unravel at a party. Unable to face people, I retired to a side room and sensed God clearly say, "You've gone away from me." His meaning was clear: it was time to return to active faith. So grateful that He had not given up on me, I fell to my knees and re-committed my life. Job done? Hardly – I was still left with the mess I had made. Sensing the opportunity, I cheekily offered to do a deal with God. I needed His help with my problems, plus I needed a particular girl – Heather – to keep me on the straight and narrow. We had gone out three years previously – another thing I had messed up. "So, God, here's the deal – you get the problems and I get the girl. Do this for me and I will never leave you again." (Not an approach to be encouraged!) Within six weeks, God had kept His side of the "bargain". Mine was to follow Him forever.

Marriage, in 1988, led to five months' voluntary medical work in India. Returning to the UK in 1989, we were taken on by the United Society for the Propagation of the Gospel (USPG) which sent us for missionary and language training, and then on to Tanzania in 1990, where we became Joint Medical Superintendents of two Anglican mission hospitals. Working in rural Tanzania was fascinating, both socially and medically, but after five years, with our oldest girl needing schooling, it was time to return home.

Back in the UK I worked for charities, then explored becoming a vicar, and finally ended up as a locum Accident and Emergency Consultant, all the while asking God what He really wanted me to do. His answer was unexpected: doors opened for a career in general practice, the very last thing I ever thought I would do. Taken on by a training practice in Teddington, Middlesex, my thoughts turned quickly to where our family should ultimately settle. In Tanzania, any time off usually led us to relax in Tanga, where we would swim in the Indian Ocean and enjoy masala prawns and a beer. So I asked God to place us at the seaside, and preferably somewhere poor, where we could make a difference. In answering, God (who creates the best networks!) gave me a strong sense that I should attend a particular training course in London. Against my trainer's advice I went, and there I met a doctor whose general practice had been looking for another Christian GP for a year. But there were two of us! Job-sharing solved the problem, and Heather and I began work in Cliftonville, Margate, in October 1998.

On our return from Africa, we had been spiritually very dry. Alpha changed everything. Recharged, I was blown away by discovering one facet of Christianity that I should have grasped years earlier – namely that "telling others" was part of the deal. Despite having become a Christian aged fourteen, and spending years as a missionary, it was not until I was thirty-seven that outreach became part of my DNA. Testing the water by speaking to just two patients in my trainee year, I vowed that when I became a proper GP, I would really go for it. Arriving in Margate, I had no idea how life-changing this inner conviction would prove to be.

Margate was indeed the poor town I had requested. Previously splendid, its many run-down hotels now housed those who had fallen on hard times. With our surgery ideally placed in this catchment area, Heather and I soon gravitated towards treating drug and alcohol addicts. Unlike the middle classes, to whom the concept of sin is often alien, addicts are usually pretty honest about their failings, and delight in doctors who show them interest rather than suspicion. Working not always comfortably with our local drug addiction agency (KCA), we began to treat this section of society in increasing numbers. Aware of the limitations of both conventional medicine and KCA, we regularly introduced the gospel as the source of personal transformation. As we did, we would discover that we were often building on faith already existing in those with a prison record, but that professing faith whilst "inside" is very different from practising it on the outside. Nevertheless, over the years we have seen many addicts come to faith, several following Alpha courses we have run in church. Not all have taken the opportunity offered and done well, however. We will always remember the names and faces of those who have died young.

Delighted that God had led us to Margate particularly to help substance abusers, we knew that the gospel was appropriate and relevant to all patients, not just those in the drug scene. The WHO has stated that health has spiritual as well as mental and physical components, and this truth is borne out in practice, with so many of our patients broken, burdened and unhealthy due to their past family and social histories. Those who have been abused are often guilty and self-harming, whilst anxiety and depression are almost endemic. Many of these patients have suffered great harm through evil intent. Antidepressants and counselling can help to an extent, and we prescribe them like any other GPs. But the spiritual aspect of so many of these conditions requires spiritual treatment. This is where the victory of Jesus over evil is seen to be very relevant. Believing passionately that only he can set people free, we have used our position as

GPs to "prescribe" him, where appropriate. This, surely, was the very reason God brought us here.

But not everyone sees Christian outreach at work in such a positive light. "What right have you as GPs to give patients something they haven't come for? How do you choose whom to 'preach' to, and what happens if they don't like it?" Others feel that whilst spiritual care may have a place, it would be better separated from the main consultation, e.g. through a chaplain attached to the surgery. Certainly, to question one's practice is healthy, but so often those who air concerns think primarily of problems that may ensue. This, to my mind, is the wrong starting point – focusing on the negatives can paralyse or lead to timidity. Instead, I would ask all Christians to put into practice the Great Commission, starting in one's own workplace – and see what happens! Delight at seeing someone respond to the gospel would then mirror ours.

Nevertheless, it is certainly true that whilst outreach within general practice has hugely enlivened our work and been significant in terms of the Kingdom, it has not been 100% problem-free. Over the years, out of literally thousands of consultations which have included a gospel element, I have personally had about eight written complaints. Patients (or more commonly a supporter not present in the consultation, but acting on their behalf) may take umbrage with the GP suggesting that whilst tablets and counselling have their place, there are things which only God can do if we let Him. All but one of these complaints have been dealt with locally, at practice or Primary Care Trust (PCT) level. Eighteen months ago, however, I received a complaint that was far nastier and went to the top.

The Case

The phone call came whilst I was on call, in early August 2010. A mother, sounding very pleasant, phoned as she was concerned about her adult son who was a patient of another GP within our practice. She had had a text from her son that suggested that he might be suicidal; she also thought that he had not received a psychological appointment. Clearly, I needed to see him as soon as possible in regard to both of these issues, but discovered that this was easier said than done as he spent most of his time in the gym. To get round this hurdle, I offered him an appointment in my evening surgery, two days later, which she accepted on his behalf.

Prior to the fateful consultation, I had never met "patient A" (as he is still referred to by legal teams) but was aware of him, having met some other members of his family. Somewhat intrigued, I familiarised myself with his case as recorded on the practice computer.

Patient "A" attended as planned. Evening surgeries take place with fixed numbers of patients and there was thus no rush. I firstly checked whether he knew why his mother had asked him to see me. He did, but was unconcerned. Aware that his situation was quite complex, I went on to emphasise that, in order to help him, I needed first to explore his past medical history in detail. My aim was to confirm the success or otherwise of treatments received thus far, before suggesting a way forward. I also mentioned at this early stage that I might approach his case from a different angle towards the end, if appropriate.

Medical confidentiality restricts what I am permitted to reveal of what took place. Essentially, however, his physical employment had come to an end through injury; in response, he had developed an exercise obsession which consumed him, and his eating disorder had worsened, which also made him depressed. Eloquently, he described the effect of his lifestyle as a form of self-abuse which had cost him his friends, and admitted that he had only been partially helped by the Eating Disorder specialists and psychologist who had treated him. Presently he was stuck, self-loathing and self-harming; but when asked why he had so alarmed his mother with his text, he was dismissive, stating that he wasn't actually suicidal and that she merely "feigned" interest in him. Having talked with him quite extensively, I agreed that he was not suicidal and documented this view within the extensive and contemporaneous notes that I was recording. The consultation so far had taken twenty minutes. At this point, presuming that he had come to me for my advice, and aware that treatments up to now had availed him little, I decided to change tack.

Knowing that he came from a family with a (non-Christian) faith background, I asked him whether his faith had proved helpful in all that had gone on. He replied that faith had mainly provided him with a community, albeit one from which he had cut himself off. Nowadays, it meant no more to him than that. With no apparent advantage provided by his faith, I asked his permission to talk about mine, receiving the affirmation, "Go for it". Accordingly, I explained how the Christian faith had greatly helped me with my problems when I was younger, and that the same applied to literally hundreds of patients who had sat in his chair; by extension, God, through Jesus, would love to help him too. He listened before becoming angry, calling me an "idiot". It was obvious that my lateral, spiritual approach was most definitely not what he thought he needed. Instead, he simply wanted more of what he had already received in terms of treatment. The consultation ended not as I would have wished it, but a degree of calm was achieved as I emphasised that I would chase up the psychological appointment that he had missed. The computer records show that we had a "faith discussion".

One of the practice secretaries was detailed to chase up his psychological appointment, and discovered that a referral had been made to a counsellor earlier that year in March. Patient "A" was duly offered an initial assessment with a Mental Health Worker but had failed to contact the service as requested. As he had failed to comply with this basic requirement of the mental health service, the appointment for 12th May 2010 did not take place. At the secretary's instigation, on my behalf and at my request, the service promised to contact him again.

Patient "A's" mother spoke to him the day after our consultation. He told her that he had poured out his heart to me in desperation to find a solution to the condition that was totally ruling his life. I agree with these comments, but take issue with his summary that I had offered him no medical help, merely Jesus. Furious, she wrote to the General Medical Council (GMC), my professional body, to complain, stating that I had been unprofessional in failing to act medically, indeed had demonstrated no medical skill and had abused a vulnerable patient by belittling his faith. There was no reference to the lengthy consultation that had taken place, nor any acknowledgement that I had undertaken the two medical tasks that she had specifically requested. Seven weeks later, patient "A" added his letter of complaint to hers and the GMC decided I had a case to answer.

In early October 2010, a thick stack of paperwork from the GMC arrived at my door. It was clear that they were taking the complaints from the patient and his mother very seriously. At first I was stunned – no-one likes receiving a complaint, particularly when one's professional body is involved. But that wasn't the half of it. The vehemence of the language used by the complainants had obviously impressed the GMC to take the case on, rather than pass it down the line to be dealt with at PCT level. By taking this step, the opportunity to resolve the problem locally (and quickly) by writing to the complainants and possibly meeting with them face to face, to clear the air, was lost. In trouble, I sought the advice of my insurance company, the Medical Protection Society (MPS).

All went quiet. Naturally, I had made my GP partners (not least my wife!) aware that there was a problem; they were very supportive and, as I was not suspended, I continued to work normally, with one caveat. With the substance of the complaint swirling around in my head, I spent much time wondering what would happen. The GMC had already put their cards on the table. After deliberating, the case would either be closed, closed with advice, a warning would be given or, worst case scenario, I would proceed to a Fitness to Practise (FTP) Panel at which my registration would be at risk.

Five months passed – plenty of time for the GMC to have looked carefully at the case and to have concluded that the complaint was both highly exaggerated and contained obvious untruths, not least in terms of my medical input in relation to the mother's specific requests. Hoping for commonsense, in truth my expectation was otherwise and I was therefore only slightly surprised to receive further correspondence from them in March 2011. The case was proceeding, it was not simply going to fade away. Stirred into action, I re-contacted the MPS, but having received their advice concerning past complaints, I knew what was coming. The MPS exists to help doctors keep their jobs. On the surface, this sounds very reasonable and I was certainly in no hurry to retire! But in practice, it meant damage limitation. Take your medicine, which in their considered view was likely to be a warning as to my future behaviour. Case over, move on. OK?

Not for me. When the MPS were proved to be correct and I duly received an official warning, I had no hesitation in rejecting it outright. Whilst this decision subsequently would receive general approval, it led to some ructions at home and raised eyebrows amongst my GP partners. Was I sure this was the right decision? Had I thought it through? Later, after my case hit the press, I would be contacted by other medics who had previously been involved with the GMC, warning me that if I took the organisation on, it would attempt to destroy me. Their plight merely increased my resolve, and having by now switched my legal team to the CLC, I was aware that the press would be involved and thus the GMC might view me less favourably. Nevertheless, I had absolutely no intention of accepting their kind offer of a warning, for a number of reasons:

Taking the warning would imply guilt, signifying that offering patient "A" the gospel as a solution to his problems had been the wrong thing to do, one that I regretted. Instead, rather than being ashamed of my actions, I had taken what I considered to have been the right course in his trying situation. To be fair, the consultation had been by no means perfect. This would have implied not only me playing my role to perfection, but that the patient did so too, in a convivial atmosphere with both parties quite content throughout. Clearly, this wasn't the case here. Nevertheless, given the same circumstances, I would offer the next patient the gospel. Why should he receive any less?

There was also a bigger picture. Right from the beginning, I was aware that mine was a test case. The GMC, in effectively accepting the complainants' points of view, viewed me as more likely guilty than innocent. What I had done, in their view, was not bad enough to justify suspension or FTP proceedings; nevertheless, my professional body was making a point: offer Christianity at your peril. Giving in (by taking the warning) would have simply encouraged the GMC and sister bodies to come down hard on the next Christian doctor, nurse, physio – whoever risked expressing their faith at work. To me, this was intolerable. Had I succumbed to what I regarded as institutional bullying, the effects would have been felt more in the future than right then.

From a personal viewpoint, a warning was not a huge deal. Sure, it would be a stain on my professional reputation for five years, and one which would need to be disclosed to any future employers; it would also act as a yellow card throughout this time, with a repeat "offence" definitely putting my job at risk. But it was not something that would keep me awake at night. For I knew how the enemy would try to discourage anyone who promoted a Christian agenda, and I could counter his wiles by recalling all the good that God has done in past consultations. In summary, I knew who my real boss was – the one before whom I would stand at the final judgment. It wasn't the GMC.

God never leaves us to fight our battles alone. In the Introduction to this book, I wrote of how I came across the CLC two years before I needed their assistance. Transferring my case to them now, I met Paul Diamond, who would become my barrister. In planning our strategy, he needed to hear my version of what took place. Of most interest was whether I had over-stepped the faith line. What exactly had I said that so upset the lad? In answer, I repeated the exact words used the previous August in clinic: "You might find that Christianity has something more to offer than your current faith." Bearing in mind that, practically speaking, he no longer subscribed to or followed this faith, my words should not logically have been seen as in any way belittling his "current" beliefs. Very likely, the GMC would see it otherwise, but this was defensible. I had received the go-ahead to talk about my faith, having already discussed his. It was therefore a conversation between two consenting adults and one that was perfectly "legal", as no GMC statute disallowed faith discussion between a doctor of one persuasion and a patient holding another view.

Was there anything else? Paul was aware – from the original complaints – that I had mentioned the devil in my presentation of faith. As a Christian, he personally had no problem with that, but could see why patient "A" had chosen to take offence here. Again, it was a question of how and why I had brought the subject up – "Please explain!" Now we had entered the realm of controversy. Not all Christians are theologically comfortable in this territory, but I am very familiar with the Bible's specific teaching on the evil one. His aims and tactics in this case seemed clear.

Condemning himself for having failed in his occupation had led Patient "A" to self-loathing and bodily harm, whilst the "blinding of his eyes" prevented him from seeing the truth. Presenting to him the concept that many of his problems could be explained through the activities of a personal force of evil, I hoped would shed light on his situation. It should also not have been a foreign concept to him, as his previous faith also made reference to evil. However, the main reason I brought the subject up was to contrast satan's intentions with those of Jesus. My message was ultimately one of hope. Many years previously, Jesus had offered me freedom from my problems. This very day patient "A" had the same opportunity before him, with abundant life thrown in, to follow. The choice was his, but one I recommended he think carefully about.

Paul's final question was equally pertinent. Did I stop there or did I bang on endlessly, as accused? My recollection is that once I had said my bit and he had made his position clear by calling me an "idiot", I simply emphasised that I really wanted to help him; please consider my offer. I certainly did not go on and on, nor did most of the consultation concern faith. If it had, there was no way that I would have been able to record the very lengthy physical and mental history that preceded our faith discussion.

Paul and I had gone over the areas which would surely come up in the hearing. We knew I had taken risks, but my motive was acceptable. As a barrister, he was only too aware of the litigious nature of modern society, and that victim behaviour is encouraged. To turn down my offer of help was the patient's right, but to talk of "abuse" and "harassment", even if my gospel presentation was less than perfect, was excessive and unreasonable. Thirty years ago, we would have agreed to disagree. Now, our little contretemps in Margate warranted national news and I was up before the beak. Before meeting the opposing barrister, however, it was important to clarify exactly what the GMC's position was concerning faith discussions.

Over the years, the GMC has tightened its regulations on the practise of faith at work. Previously, the organisation had taken the view that faith discussion between doctor and patient can take place, as long as it is done sensitively (shades of 1 Peter 3:15, reflecting the input of the Christian Medical Fellowship in formulating the statutes.) More recently, however, regulations have tightened – doctors should not now normally present their personal views unless they are directly relevant to a patient's case. Still sound in theory, my case has shown that in practice any doctor taking a spiritual history and discussing faith with a patient risks being disciplined and possibly sanctioned if a problem arises. By taking this stance, the GMC not only betrays its position with regard to Christianity, but does so flying in the face of evidence.

There are now thousands of papers examining the effects of faith on health. The huge majority of these have looked solely at Christianity, with more than 80% recording improvements in mental and physical health – with even cancer and response to surgery influenced by God's touch. Christians even live longer! By ignoring such an evidence-base and merely concentrating on the occasional problem, the GMC performs a considerable disservice to the patients it claims to be serving; just imagine, for comparison, an orthopaedic surgeon being prevented from replacing hips if just 1 in 100 operations developed a complication – rightly, there would be an outcry. Why should "whole person medicine", in which the spiritual health of the patient is tackled, be treated any differently?

We had considered our position in relation to expression of faith at work. Simply maintaining this freedom would have made my struggle with the GMC worthwhile. But I was very keen that other aspects of the case were not simply glossed over. Central to her accusation, the patient's mother stated that I had been unprofessional and demonstrated no medical expertise. Even a brief perusal of the notes would have shown this claim to be false, as a clear, accurate and lengthy history was evident, and the psychological appointment had been chased up as a matter of urgency. Why did the GMC simply choose to ignore such obvious facts, focusing their ire on purely subjective opinions?

In English law, complainants' arguments must be accurate or they risk being thrown out. With such blatant inaccuracies, the organisation had ample opportunity *de novo* to dismiss the case outright. The fact that they did not do so and pursued me doggedly, despite the evidence, led me to two conclusions. Firstly, my professional body, which I had mistakenly assumed existed to serve the best interests of doctors as well as patients, instead was consumer-driven.

Secondly, and of much more concern, it has a strong secular agenda, and was inherently biased against doctors who are also Christians.

We were ready for the first hearing, which took place in the GMC offices in Manchester in late September 2011. Two of my former drug addict patients who had become Christians attended to testify on my behalf but, like myself, were not permitted to speak as only the opposing barristers batted legal arguments back and forth. The argument centred around whether the key witness – the patient himself – should attend. Having penned a note to say that he would not do so even if paid a million pounds, it was clear that he would not do so voluntarily! In a criminal court, a no-show by the witness would lead to the case being struck out. Mr Diamond insisted that this should be the case, as the complainants' letters amounted to no more than "hearsay" without the opportunity for cross-examination to establish the truth of the matter. Countering this, the opposing barrister indicated that, even if the hearing did take this view, he had enough ammunition to proceed, using transcripts of radio interviews I had given after the case hit the press.

The chair of the independent panel presiding over the hearing now had a problem. With the defendant (myself) present and willing to be cross-examined by the GMC's barrister, it would only be right and proper if the complainant acted likewise. In his absence, should she view the written complaints as hearsay, thus concluding the case, or apply a lower standard of justice in these quasi-judicial proceedings? No doubt aware of the heavy press interest, she chose the latter option, merely asking the GMC to try again to persuade patient "A" to attend. The matter was adjourned, quite unsatisfactorily, with a provisional date for another hearing in the spring.

As we filed out of the building, Andrea was especially

livid. She explained the implication of what had just transpired. In resolutely pursuing me on the basis of unsubstantiated hearsay, the GMC had effectively abrogated its responsibility to defend doctors from any wild allegations made by patients. Far from protecting doctors, no doctor was now safe; like teachers accused of misbehaviour by pupils, we were now guilty until proved innocent. A very sad day for our profession.

Months passed, during which patient "A" now agreed to testify, but only by telephone. This was his best offer, consistent with maintaining his anonymity and confidentiality at all times. Unsurprisingly, our team was nonplussed, as such restriction of access usually only applies in cases involving violence or sexual abuse, neither of which, as far as I was aware, took place in my surgery! With our side still not given a fair crack of the whip, Mr Diamond again asked for the case to be struck out; the panel would ultimately decide otherwise, and my feeling that a second hearing in Manchester would be necessary would prove prescient. All doom and gloom? Hardly.

I always knew that transferring my case to Christian Concern meant likely press involvement, but had no practical idea of what this would entail. In May 2011, the London office put the word out to selected journalists who were trusted to report fairly and without negative bias. The story spread like wildfire, just as Andrea had hoped. Christian Concern are no shrinking violets, majoring on the truth writ large and in lights. Where Christians are being marginalised, especially at work, the organisation uses and indeed relies on the media to make public such behaviour. Unfair judgments are now no longer kept below the radar and swept under the carpet, but are in the open for scrutiny. In my case, this has led to two very positive sequelae. Firstly, awareness has led not only to information but debate. Articles in newspapers and journals, added to the many radio interviews, have led to much discussion and comment in the form of letters and emails from the public. The case was even discussed in a medical ethics class at Bristol University. Overwhelmingly the response has been very positive, and not just from Christians. Other faiths, including the Muslims in Margate, have been right behind me, as have many non-believers whose interest is in freedom of speech and a doctor's right to help patients in whatever way he or she sees fit. The main dissenting voices have come, not unexpectedly, from the National Secular Society who proved to be the source behind the radio transcripts used by the GMC!

Secondly and even more gratifyingly, the support I have received from Christians around the world has been stunning. Hundreds of letters have been written to me directly, with others reaching me via the GMC. All but three have been hugely supportive. The Bible states that when one part of the body suffers, the whole body is involved. With letters from as far as Hawaii and Australasia, this was certainly borne out. Others emailed me their support, having seen articles written in their national newspapers in India and Uganda. Patients, too, have commented on my case. Pleased that I have not been suspended and that I am therefore able to continue working, many are outraged and make the point that the very name of our practice, Bethesda Medical Centre, gives a strong clue to the Christian ethos within! Backed up by our plasma screen stating that any patient not wishing to discuss spiritual issues will have his views respected, many of my non-Christian patients were at a loss to understand what the problem was. If patient "A" didn't like what we offered, why did he not simply say so or take his custom elsewhere?

So many positives, but the downside was that the GMC's application of their own unique rules allowed the case to continue despite the absence in person of the complainant. The second hearing date planned for the spring was cancelled after I needed treatment for bowel cancer, diagnosed towards the end of 2011. By June 2012, with surgery and radiotherapy completed, and suffering few side effects from IV and oral chemotherapy, I was ready. This time, the GMC allocated a full four days for the hearing, a statement of intent if ever there was one that the show was going ahead, with or without the key witness – patient "A".

Prior to the hearing, I knew of the importance of winning this case. Not all Christians are naturally bold in witnessing at work, and losing might discourage them further. So I prayed that God would both soften hearts within the panel and that He would put a Christian in place to work on behalf of myself, my team and others in the health profession who might be in my position in the future. And He did. Right from the start, the chairman of the panel presented his credentials as an evangelical Christian. Naturally there was no objection from us, nor was there from the opposing barrister, who following the conclusion of the case would also declare himself to be a churchgoer. Two for the price of one! Thank you, Lord, but how would they shape up in practice? I didn't have to wait long to find out.

Having declared his faith, the panel chair then bent over backwards to be excessively "fair" to the GMC counsel. Immediately prior to the hearing, the counsel had presented an email sent that morning from the patient's GP, one of my partners, stating that the patient was now too unwell to attend. The evidence that in the previous nine months the GMC had made strenuous attempts to secure his attendance was minimal, and bearing in mind his previous statement that one million pounds would not persuade him otherwise, this claim was disputed by our team. Where was the psychiatric report accompanying such a statement? Equally, the excellent GP had almost certainly been leant on by the patient and GMC to provide a statement at the last minute without being fully aware of the consequences for our team. Nevertheless, the panel chairman was content that sufficient effort had been made and that patient "A" should be allowed to testify in private, anonymously and by telephone.

This was extraordinary. My counsel, Mr Diamond, had already summarised why a complainant needed to be cross-examined in person under English law. He could also find no precedent in the UK where evidence by telephone had been deemed sufficient, a point not disputed by his opposing number. We also questioned whether the patient's views concerning his health were correct and not merely convenient. But our logic was simply dismissed. In retrospect and being charitable, maybe the chairman thought that his own personal faith required him to be biased towards the opposite side and that that was how Christians should act in these circumstances. But whatever his thoughts, the obvious warmth between himself and both the GMC counsel and patient "A" was most certainly not extended towards our team. Instead, we sensed an unusual degree of hostility from the panel and considered walking out of the hearing room towards the end of the second day, sensing this was no fair "trial".

To use a football analogy, we were 3-0 down by the end of day two, and although my cross-examination the next day went reasonably well, the judgment found entirely in the patient's favour on the last day. We were walked all over, with the patient having been found to be a credible witness, despite being unable to recall whether the consultation lasted five or twenty-five minutes. Furthermore, our pleas concerning the complainant's fabrication that nothing medical had taken place in the consultation were ignored. Finally, even though he had walked out and thus terminated the discussion, I was found not to have put a plan in place for the future. Whilst some of the allegations were not "proven", several were and, to cap it all, I was called evasive in reference to remembering two details of the consultation which had taken place nearly two years previously. If that was the case, how much more evasive was the complainant who could not even be bothered to give evidence in person!

The result, as the GMC always intended, was a formal warning on my record for the next five years. But there was more to come. As an unwanted extra, the local Primary Care Trust chose to get involved. Convening a meeting with me six months later, in December 2012, which by their own admission was not essential, the intention ostensibly was to check that I would abide by the GMC ruling. Having learnt that I would, the real reason for the meeting became clear. Any faith-based complaint received within the five-year period, no matter how trivial, must be made known to them. With assistance from the Local Medical Committee (LMC), this "sentence" was reduced to two years, but the meaning was clear. Instead of having to wait for a major complaint to attract the attention of our highest medical authority, any unhappiness, no matter how small, if related to a faith discussion in surgery, would now lead to a chain reaction in which our practice manager would be obliged to inform the PCT, triggering a sequence of events leading to a Fitness to Practise Hearing at the GMC, with my job at risk.

I don't know why God allowed us to lose this particular battle, but I am convinced that we will be able to look back in three years and understand better what He was up to! One thing I am clear about, however, is the identity of the real enemy here: not the mother, nor the son or even the GMC; not the National Secular Society or any others delighted by my "misfortune" – rather, the evil one, who has had a go; pleasingly, in my view, he has done himself absolutely no good whatsoever, regardless of the unsatisfactory "legal" outcome. Public debate and massive support have led his attempt to discredit and demoralise this Christian to fail utterly. The important thing has been remembering to love and pray for my human opponents, mentioned above.

Many people have asked me one simple question: with all that you have gone through, do you still talk to patients about God? The answer is easy! This spring (2013), I was asked to bring a team of medics, nurses and therapists to Saclepea, Liberia. Before dealing with the sick, we preached the gospel to the assembled patients each morning. One man stood up. On behalf of his fellow Liberians, he thanked us for not neglecting their spiritual needs, and rejoiced that we hoped to pray for patients as well as to prescribe for them. And the situation is no different here in the UK. In the last month, I have prayed for a man dying from cancer and seen a lady with severe anxiety and depression beaming with joy, having plucked up courage to join our current Alpha Course in church. Many of the drug addicts we treat are also on Alpha, and one already wants to be baptised. Another lady in her mid-thirties, close to death from alcoholism, has responded to medical input and prayer from her wider family and can't wait to come back to church. The list goes on. Why would I want to stop now, when there is so much work to do and God is clearly not asleep on the job.

Undoubtedly, the last two years or so have taken a toll, particularly on my wife, Heather, who has hated the GMC business with a passion. It has also affected me physically. Stress, through its effect on the immune system, has been shown to increase the chance of malignancy, and being a doctor merely meant that I ignored for longer than I should have done the warning signs of which I was aware! Rectal cancer is not to be recommended, but the Lord has been very gracious and allowed me to remain pretty healthy throughout the surgery, radiotherapy and chemotherapy which have taken up much of the last year. Strong faith has proved handy in fighting for my health as well as for the right to speak out at work. As ever, all things work together for good for those who love God.

What does the future hold for me? Publishing this book has encouraged me that my second book, *Oh God! I've got Cancer*, will see the light of day. Missions – medical and otherwise – remain a joy, and with our last child leaving home this summer, Heather and I should have more time together to indulge our love of active holidays. But whilst I have the energy, I would be a fool to walk away from my calling to reach out spiritually to my patients. They continue to matter to God, and even though the GMC regularly tightens guidelines on good medical conduct, I refuse to be discouraged from practising good medicine which must include looking after the spiritual health of my patients. My hope is that others will not be put off by the prevailing climate, and will do so too.

10

Christina Summers
The City Councillor

Christina spent much of her first two years of life in an orphanage, knowing nothing of her natural father, and her unmarried mother was in prison. Thankfully, God has a soft spot for orphans, and placed her, at the age of two and a half, in a family with an older brother whom she adored and who became her best friend. The feeling was mutual, for he had chosen her to be his little sister, probably due to her cute blonde, curly hair and a tomboy nature which enabled her to kick anything, including footballs. Indeed, on being introduced to her foster mother she kicked her in the shin! Allied to being able to talk for Britain, it might be assumed that the young Christina was an extrovert, but the reverse was the case – she was extremely shy with an aversion to eye contact, leading to a downward gaze. But at night in the orphanage she had barely slept – wandering around, she supposes, looking for someone to talk to.

Growing up, Christina struggled with issues of identity and rejection, and also fought with her adoptive father. If unfairly treated, as she was on a regular basis, her indignation was so loud and animated that any verbal or physical abuse coming her way led to all hell breaking out. An innate sense of justice was thus apparent from an early age as she was incapable of controlling her fury at unfairness. This trait has remained with her into adulthood, although God has removed the quick temper (with its propensity to cause collateral damage!) and trained her in self-control.

Thankfully, throughout all this trauma she was comforted by her Italian mother. With a most tender heart and affection, this godly woman was so full of grace that Christina could not imagine anyone more perfect on this earth under God, with whom her mother most definitely had a relationship. When war was declared with her father, she acted as Christina's protector, and when cancer took her away when Christina was twenty-five, it tore her apart. Good people die, but she was great. However, God had already stepped in and taken control of the situation. Through her sister-in-law, she had come across the Christian family of a work colleague who embraced her as one of their own. The father was an amazing, quietly confident man of God, who spoke plainly about the truth. A year or so later, after reasoning with him, she submitted herself to Jesus Christ, and by faith became a new creation.

God had revealed Himself to her in a reasoned way, and that is how she talks about her faith when asked. In doing so, she has had to overcome her shyness, for it took her some years to begin to enjoy toying with the limelight and participating in apologetics in public. Following her business degree in Brighton and in Turin, Italy, in the 1990s, there was little clue as to the direction in which God would eventually lead her as she undertook many unrelated jobs. It was not until the year 2000 that she became involved in the kind of work that once again stirred up the spirit within her to fight against injustice on behalf of the vulnerable. Working alongside another Christian in Brighton, she helped run a street ministry which has developed over the last decade and become a serious partner with the council in tackling issues of homelessness, addiction, housing, etc. Then for a few years she tried various business ventures as well as training in radio news broadcasting, including a short stint at the BBC World Service. She then revisited community work and campaigning, which directed her towards her local Green councillors in late 2008.

Immediately, she was struck by their willingness to engage with and encourage their constituents, allied to a determination to do the right thing for them, even if on paper it appeared impossible. "Where there's a will, there's a way" seemed to be the unspoken maxim of the Green representatives. Loving their fighting spirit, she began to attend full council meetings as well as other committees, asking questions on behalf of various community groups. It was an eye-opener into the world of Green politicians and activists. She was not only impressed by their debate and relevance but also by the way in which they conducted themselves. Eschewing personal attacks on the opposition, arguments were well thought through, with good humour and little hot air. She felt that the Greens spoke good sense, were action-orientated, and overall good value for her council tax!

Impressed with their spirit, she also valued their friendliness as social opportunities came her way. But she now had to consider their policies, their principles and their thinking. How did these sit with the faith that was fundamental to her identity and which she was not, therefore, prepared to keep private? Essentially, would their policies contradict or complement her biblical Christian position?

She began to examine environmental issues. Convinced that in this area she had hitherto been negligent, Bible study rapidly showed her that bad stewardship of God's provision is a serious thing, and that in messing up the natural world, people are messed up too, with the most vulnerable being hit the hardest. No wonder environmentalists are such passionate people! Caroline Lucas, the 2010 prospective parliamentary candidate who was to become the first Green

MP, then hosted an event for the community at Christina's church. What she (and others) said about the economy in relation to the environment made good logical sense to her. At one time, such concern had chiefly been expressed at European Union level. But the Greens, whilst aware of the dangers presented to Britain by this seemingly unstoppable monster, aimed at participating and winning arguments rather than simply protesting and pulling out. She got their point and decided to trust Caroline Lucas MEP, whose experience in Europe was immeasurably greater than hers.

Christina took to local Green politics like a duck to water. An innate activist, she understood the principles behind Green thinking, and began to imagine how her city might be transformed. Having already accumulated experience in the areas of transport, air quality, policing and crime, she desperately wanted to know more about the environment at local level. Working with the Greens – and even conceivably representing the party – felt like a real opportunity to learn about and implement things she had missed out on after years of focusing on people *per se*, rather than the authorities that govern them.

So, having received some encouragement from serving Green councillors with whom she had formed some really good friendships, she agreed to stand in the 2011 local elections. Even though within the party she was aware of a few rumblings about her assumed Christian stance on the more sensitive issues (not least homosexuality), Christina felt sure that she would prove herself as a councillor and very active party member. Having joined the party in October 2009, she immediately helped in the General Election campaign, right up to Caroline's victory. Almost immediately she was in campaign mode again, first for a by-election and then for her own campaign. Trusted even as a relative newcomer to act as Joint Election Co-ordinator, it was a testing experience. Unexpected success led her to work hard for the first UK Green administration, particularly promoting better internal relationships, communication and ways of working. In general, she had no difficulty in working with her other twenty-two colleagues in trying to fulfil a very exciting and visionary local manifesto, but she was aware that there were significant differences of opinion, and even conflict. Personally, she thought this was likely to manifest around the lesbian-gay issue, but she felt that in good conscience she could comfortably abstain from voting on these matters on grounds of equality as she understood it and God's love for all humanity.

But she was wrong. In little more than a year into her post, Christina would be expelled from the party after disagreeing on a clear issue of conscience that should never have been on a council agenda, and on which she had never campaigned.

The Case

The trigger for what subsequently took place occurred in February 2012. Christina joined a Christian friend outside Wistons, an abortion clinic on Dyke Road, Brighton, in order to pray for clients and the staff. She did this "off-duty" (i.e. in her own time and therefore neither as a city councillor, nor as a Green Party member or representative). This was one of two visits she paid to the clinic – the previous one having been with a group of people, one evening after closing hours a few days earlier. But it was the second visit that attracted attention, after a photo of her was posted the following day on Twitter.

Green colleagues pounced on the picture instantly, and a major storm blew up, both within the Green Group and the local party. The opposition she received from colleagues was ostensibly on the grounds of having risked bringing the party into disrepute. The backlash and vilification she received would have serious consequences, but it was nevertheless not an issue that ever became public – in spite of fears to the contrary – nor did it ever need to. Most unfortunately, however, small elements of the story would emerge in a blog, and would later be used by the disciplinary panel that contributed towards her expulsion from the Green Group of councillors later that year.

Returning to February 2012 – despite Christina's appeals, standard practice in the Green Party led to the issues not being promptly dealt with and dying down, with "normal" life resuming, albeit with fractured relationships within the group and party. But one thing was clear: the incident had brought to the surface a violent prejudice against her as a Christian, labelling her in some colleagues' minds as homophobic, a hatred-stirrer and an underminer of women's rights, etc. In retrospect, it was therefore hardly surprising that things would come to a head at the July meeting of the full council, chaired by the mayor, Green councillor Bill Randall, who had stepped down as council leader in May.

A week or so before the full council met on 19th July 2012, councillors were supplied with the intended agenda, including any Notices of Motion that the political parties might want to table. This is simply a way of presenting a wider, more national issue for debate and voting. Labour at this time chose to table a Notice of Motion supporting the government's plans for same-sex marriage. This was not something Christina felt she could possibly support or even abstain on, in view of the enormous practical and spiritual implications. She knew the Greens would be totally in favour and that this was a serious decision for her to make, with huge consequences. She initially talked to her church fellowship, all of whom are actively spiritually engaged in the city's affairs, and also warned the council leader that she could not support this motion and, indeed, would not only vote against it but would also speak to it, to clarify her personal position. In other words, she would exercise her right to freedom of speech in a party that does not operate a whipping system (in theory giving each Green councillor freedom to express their view, even if it differs from the party line, and to vote according to conscience). She also ensured she followed Green party protocol by making absolutely clear what the party's view was on this issue.

Sadly, the council leader did not wish her to object at full council, and alerted the rest of the Green Group to her position. Receiving strong support from several others, and on the back of the February incident, it was generally felt that whilst party members are not whipped, it was non-negotiable that same-sex marriage was an issue of equality because this was, they claimed, a fundamental tenet of Green policy and values. Christina's objection would therefore be seen by the whole party as a rebellion against all that it stood for.

From that point on, she was constantly pressed to reconsider, and either to abstain or to leave the council chamber during the debate. After much wrestling, praying and discussion with her church fellowship and friends, however, Christina decided that the price was worth paying. The family order of God (in the marriage covenant) has been under violent attack in our nation in recent years, not least in Brighton, which is at the very heart of this rebellion. She had been aware since her election that, in this season in the public realm, her role is to make a stand for righteousness and to demonstrate Kingdom principles, a position she felt that the church in Brighton had failed in, preferring to partner with ungodly authority on a ticket of appeasement, using the concept of grace as a justification. She was convicted that her role was to be like that of Esther and Daniel, taking hold of God's Law and bringing it to the highest place of government in the city.

Amongst the flurry of emails received from colleagues days before full council was a threat that if she went ahead with her intended actions, if she was not expelled from the party as a result, there would be a good number who would step down from the administration. Then, the day before the full council met, Christina agreed to an emergency meeting with Caroline Lucas MP, at her request. Christina's position and the likely consequences were discussed. Christina was asked to consider abstaining, or leaving the chamber, but no pressure was applied and Caroline understood her position of conscience. Indeed, she communicated her support to the Green Group and the wider party for Christina's right to exercise her conscience, for which she attracted some opposition.

On full council day, aware that colleagues were anxious about what she was planning to do, that they would wish to deter her in every way, Christina did not attend the usual pre-council meeting in which the agenda was dissected and voting strategy decided upon. There would be no point – there was already bad feeling and she did not wish to feel bullied into backing down or watering down her speech. This was far too crucial an issue to allow herself to be tethered. But at God's prompting she did see the Head of Law within the council (who sits next to and assists the Mayor), forewarning him about her intended actions and explaining her Christian stance, which greatly impressed him.

Within the chamber, with tensions high, she was ignored by most of her colleagues. With much prolonged anticipation, the same-sex marriage debate eventually came up at 10 p.m, with the Greens putting forward an amended version to tighten protection for churches. The debate then took place, with Christina the first councillor to respond, but only after the Head of Law caught her indicating to speak and informed the Mayor. She was followed by other Green, Tory and Labour councillors. As a result of her actions, the party's communications officer issued a statement on the local website. In it, the party emphasised that she had been the only councillor out of 23 voting against civil marriage for same sex couples. Her Christian faith was mentioned, and a quote from the Deputy Leader of the council, who identified himself as gay, stated that Greens have always been the party most positive about same sex marriage, and that while Christina had a long-standing position of conscience based on her faith, this did not represent the position, spirit or track record of the party in extending human and civil rights for all social groups irrespective of sexual orientation or on other grounds. He went on to say that Green councillors do not have a whip and on matters of conscience are permitted to vote freely, and that they would be meeting again soon to discuss this issue further.

As expected, the next day Christina received several emails from party members and voters, expressing horror at her betrayal and calling for her resignation. When she stood as a candidate she had signed an agreement stating that she was committed to upholding equality for all people, regardless of sexual orientation and religion – and thus had gone against Green party policy. This was a disciplinary offence.

That same day she was contacted by a senior reporter of the Argus (regional newspaper), who covers full council meetings. Having a good relationship with him, she was able to explain her Christian stance on marriage, and the need to make a stand. In speaking to him, though, she knew she had broken the party's protocol in not seeking leadership approval prior to engaging with the media. But, by this stage, statements were issued against her on social media so she felt justified in clarifying her position. Naturally, having done so, she received a strong email of disapproval from the Deputy Leader.

On 21st July 2012, the Argus story broke. Many of the party members are LGBT and were thus extremely angry, not only with her, but also with the fact that she was permitted to be a Green councillor in the first place. One particular member has been very public and campaigned against her, blogging his unqualified objections against her, and starting a public campaign to have her removed from the public arena if the party did not throw her out first.

The following week, the Green Group resolved to set up a disciplinary panel to investigate whether her actions effectively acted to renege on the equality statement she had signed before being elected. Amazingly, included in this resolution was a recommendation that the panel should conclude that she had done so, and thus dismiss her!

For her part, Christina contacted the Christian Legal Centre (CLC). Many media interviews ensued as a result, while disciplinary proceedings were put in place. The disciplinary panel hearing took place on 13th August 2012. Accompanied by a member of the CLC, the panel should have comprised the local party chair, a Green Group moderator and the council leader, but mysteriously the latter did not attend. Reasons given for his non-attendance were inconsistent, and later she learned (on Twitter!) that he had stepped down from the panel. The remaining panel members, however, insisted that, had he remained, they would still have drawn the same conclusions and recommendations.

On 10th September, the panel presented its findings to the Green Group, recommending that she be expelled on grounds of a "pattern of behaviour" that brought the party into disrepute – not because of the equality statement, which was clearly insufficient grounds on which to expel her. On

17th September, amidst a media storm, her Green Group colleagues voted 13:9 to expel her. From the council's CEO, she received on 20th September official notice of the expulsion, which granted her immediate status as an independent.

With help from the CLC an appeal against this decision was made to the national Green Party on twelve grounds. On 19th October she attended the appeal hearing. During proceedings, the three disciplinary panel members were fair and attentive, but unfortunately had invited the Chair of the previous panel. Nevertheless, she left the proceedings with some degree of hope. But, sadly, on 19th November, she was told that her appeal had been dismissed on all grounds. All that was left for her to do was to decide whether to appeal against the whole party for a breach of human rights.

Approaching the end of 2012, with her case by no means settled or finished, Christina was finding it difficult simply to "move on". With so many injustices having been committed by the Green Party, including much spin to the media, the activist within her could not let that go unchallenged. What had affected her personally also had wider public and political implications. Resonating deep within her was the truth from Proverbs that, "Righteousness exalts a nation, but sin condemns any people" – and she had desired to see a righteous government for as long as she could remember. So it was particularly tragic to see something worthwhile within the Green political arena so quickly snuffed out. The new politics they sincerely claimed to embrace, when tested in a position of power, turned out to be propelled by self-centred individualism, and even narcissism. With hindsight, this should come as no surprise, as the party is at best vaguely tolerant of religion, and at worst uncompromisingly intolerant of any dissent on issues of life and identity. "Totalitarianism", Christina insists, is no unwarranted hyperbole here. Speaking the truth means saying it as it really is in order to bring conviction and not, as many have accused, simply to cause offence. Jesus was full of grace and truth – not one or the other, but both.

The Greens, far from being a breath of fresh air politically, have shown themselves to be self-serving by forcing their own set of moral codes upon the majority for the sake of an aggrieved and bully-like minority. This is neither democracy nor a just way to govern. Sadly, churches have not done well either. In her city an opportunity was missed to demonstrate what *godly* government ought to be like, not only defending the poor, weak and vulnerable (as it does) but also standing up to be counted when one of its own is treated with such contempt on a crucial issue of conscience. The church, collectively, chose to distance itself from the fight. Jesus said, "If the world hates you, know that it has hated me before it hated you." But the body of Christ here just could not bear being hated. Favour of man was evidently placed before God's favour and, in Christina's eyes, the church had joined the Green Party in disrepute in this matter. Saddened by her Green colleagues, her greatest disappointment was in being let down by the church that bears Christ's name.

But, thankfully, God's purposes prevail. He called her into government and made her an activist, but how does that now look? As an independent councillor, it has been a relief to step back from party politics for a season and focus solely on the ward she was elected to serve. Reflecting over the past months, and waiting on the Lord, has reassured her that her removal from the Green Group of councillors was not in vain but an act of grace, as she has watched the group reap what they have sown. Becoming increasingly divided as a minority administration, she saw the last leader re-elected by just a single vote. In contrast, she is able to speak freely without being punished by party machinery – freedom indeed! Moreover, she has also been greatly encouraged by the many messages received from opposition councillors and the general public locally and nationally, who have praised her integrity in resisting political expediency and popularity, and for holding her ground on an issue of conscience.

But what to do practically? Initially, she and the CLC had six months in which to mount a full legal case against both the local and national Green Party. The chances of success would be no more than 50:50 but the barrister, Paul Diamond, would base his case on two main arguments: that the party did not follow "due process" before, during and following the disciplinary hearing, and that they discriminated on the grounds of a protected characteristic as defined in the Equality Act 2010 (religion/conscience).

Over the first quarter of 2013, Christina decided to press ahead with the legal case as she had had no clear direction from God to proceed otherwise. However, listening to His promptings is crucial too. Paul's journeying took sudden and unexpected twists and turns, and Christina, too, sensed an abrupt change in direction and strategy towards the end of March 2013. The reasons are threefold.

Firstly, the great favour afforded to her by all kinds of people as a result of the Greens' actions would be undermined if taking them to court appeared like an act of revenge. Instead, she should cultivate this favour as she works out her future in politics.

Secondly, in the light of their serious internal division, she would be wise to leave the Greens to work out their own end – without interference and the risk of uniting them in a legal battle.

Lastly, God gives us grace and authority, but we cannot exercise the latter outside the sphere into which we are called. Doing so, without His authority may make us vulnerable to becoming a casualty. Within her sphere of government she believes she rightly fought the battles that presented themselves and stood for truth. In a different (legal) sphere, she would not have the same spiritual authority and might face the same outcome as the seven sons of Sceva in Acts chapter 19, whose authority the demon did not recognise! Instead, she should continue to confront the Green Party's appalling actions, particularly with respect to equality, within her given realm of government. If she is correct, and God is honoured in this new direction, she has no doubt that He will present her with the right time and opportunity to deal with the Green Party. God will not be mocked.

As to the future, she has been asked many times whether she will stand again in the 2015 elections. Unable to answer yet, she does not feel that her political career will be fulfilled within local government. There is more to come. She loves Brighton (and Hove), and even though it has been labelled the most godless city in the UK, it is not beyond the reach of God to turn it around, and part of that process will, no doubt, involve the removal of ungodly government. We worship a God who is no respecter of political parties, and who is able to touch the hearts and minds of politicians across the political spectrum everywhere. But the bigger picture involves her deep yearning for Britain to turn back to God, and for His righteousness to prevail in our national government. Since she presumes to worship a God for whom the nations are like a drop in a bucket, she will not presume to limit her call.

PART FIVE

SHARING FAITH ON THE STREET

11

Michael Overd
The Street Preacher

Michael is in his late forties and spent his early life in a small village just outside Taunton in Somerset. Dragged along to Sunday School in his mother's Baptist church, he would rather have spent the time playing with friends but recognises that perhaps a small gospel seed was planted during that period. But the seed grew slowly as it wasn't until 2005 that he was born again. Prior to then he had been a paratrooper which had led him to become proud, selfish, arrogant and violent, because physically he was much stronger than the average man. Who needed God when he was that fit? It took a chronic back condition to lead him to repentance and faith in his Saviour.

On being saved, it didn't take him long to see that the greatness of God was not being reflected in the Christianity he saw around him. Right from the start he was very zealous to preach. The first time he did so was in the DIY department of B&Q store on the outskirts of Taunton. Approaching the checkouts, he had an incredible desire to share the Good News with all the people queuing up to pay. On the heels of this desire, though, came fear and the thought that no way would he do this in reality. Little did he know where his Lord would take him and what He would eventually have him doing.

Spending a little time with a local pastor/street preacher

helped Michael learn the ropes before he and his wife Rachel stepped out on to the streets of Taunton in June 2009. This is a place he would hardly have chosen to work had he not felt a specific calling from Jesus to do so! He normally preaches at the same spot on the High Street on alternate Saturdays plus once during the week. He has also preached in Exeter and Glastonbury on occasion, and is supported in his work by his wife at weekends, and by other Christians, who may also take turns to preach.

Rachel reports that during these three-hour slots Michael will speak for thirty minutes, using a hand-held microphone and referring to boards displaying Bible verses. He uses everyday language to explain the passages, and often gives out leaflets to passers-by. Not everybody appreciates what he does, and many walk past because the Bible message may be on subjects like sin and repentance, which offends some people. Some will stop to listen, which encourages him, but others can be very aggressively opposed, and this can lead to threats of violence. Nevertheless, when asked what he gains personally from preaching, Michael replies that he does so out of obedience to the Saviour, hoping that even a single soul will be saved as a result.

The events of 23rd October, 2010
Michael and Rachel arrived in Taunton at midday, meeting five other street preachers. They set up in the usual way. Three of the others preached in addition to Michael, and they gave out leaflets to passers-by. At the time of the incident, Michael was preaching from 1 Corinthians 6:9–10, which describes qualifications for heaven and mentions sinful practices, e.g. theft, greed, and those practising sexual immorality, including adultery and homosexuality. At this point two men, holding hands, walked past Rachel then turned around to walk back towards Michael. Michael did not

speak directly to the men as they came nearer but continued to preach. As they approached, they started shouting and stood in front of him, close to his face and almost leaning over him.

The incident lasted about thirty seconds, during which the men were very aggressive, threatening to beat Michael up, calling him names and using other foul language as well as asking who the hell he thought he was to speak in this way. They also kissed each other, distressing the daughter of one of Michael's friends when they did so. Michael remained calm but genuinely thought he would be assaulted for the first time ever whilst preaching. One of the other male street preachers began to walk towards him when he saw the confrontation, but then the men walked away. Not once had Michael ever singled them out in his preaching, and indeed he managed to carry on speaking for a little longer before talking to a flower seller who had a stall near where they preached, and who was very upset by what had taken place. Just then the men appeared again, cursed and swore, and one of them spat at Michael, but missed his target. That shook him yet further, but he continued what he was doing, finishing as usual about 3 p.m. Michael was very shaken by what had taken place but recognised in the men the same violent streak that he had before being saved.

The events of 16th July, 2011

Michael and Rachel had again gone to Taunton town centre, but it was raining and they lacked amplification or Scripture boards. They began by offering Christian leaflets to passers-by before Rachel returned to their car as she was feeling unwell. Michael then began to preach on the forgiveness of sins. At this point, the two men who had been aggressive to him the previous October walked straight towards him. Seeing them, Michael remembers saying words to the effect of: *"even these dear chaps here, these dear men caught in homosexuality, if they ask God for forgiveness of sin they can be forgiven their sins, God loves them that much."* At this point, the men took offence to a greater degree than previously, not only repeating their threats to beat him up but also going into graphic detail about what they do with each other, and saying who was he to judge whether that's right or wrong? Michael replied, appealing to them on the basis of God's love on the cross but stopped, as it was just making matters worse; the men became wilder and were joined suddenly by several others who had opposed Michael's message in the past and appeared as if from nowhere to aggressively oppose him too.

Now the situation was becoming increasingly serious. Michael finished his message and gave out some tracts while one of the men called the police. Michael packed his bags but was too scared to return to the car park as it was isolated. Telling his wife by phone to remain with the car, he left, walking towards a shop. The men determined to follow him. Thankfully, they didn't perform a citizens' arrest on him as the police had advised against it, but they did begin to accuse Michael of sexually abusing children and being a "kiddie fiddler". At this point, Michael himself threatened to call the police; this made them back off a bit, and then one of the men agreed to allow Michael to speak to the police. A car was sent and, as it arrived, Michael ran towards it, requesting they take him to the station for his own safety. They did so before releasing him and asking his wife to take him home, which she did as Michael was too shaken to drive.

A week later, Michael was arrested by the Avon and Somerset police and charged under the Public Order Act. The Act states that, "a person is guilty of an offence if he uses threatening, abusive or insulting words or behaviour, within the hearing or sight of a person likely to be caused harassment, alarm or distress thereby. An offence under this section may be committed in a public or private place." Before being charged, he was offered but refused to take a caution – as doing so would be tantamount to admitting guilt for his actions. This in turn would make it very difficult for either himself or other street preachers in the future. In addition to talking about the two events, he was asked about his preaching and the reaction of people generally to what he did. He admitted that he sometimes directed what he said at certain people, but indicated that he had not singled these men out initially in October 2010. He went on to say that sometimes people do take his words personally, through guilt and the conscience given to us by God, but that on other occasions when he had spoken on subjects like drunkenness, those that are homeless and drunk don't come to beat him up or threaten to kill him.

He then mentioned that he very rarely spoke about homosexuality, and Rachel confirmed that in 2½ years of open air work, she had never heard him say that homosexuals would burn in hell. Nevertheless, Michael agreed that homosexuality, sex before marriage and abortion were wrong, and that hell is a place where non-believers end up, in line with biblical teaching.

When then asked whether he was more mindful of what he was preaching when he saw gay people, he replied that he only preached what the Bible says, and appealed to all sinners. When pushed to explain whether he wanted them to change to become heterosexuals, Michael replied that that was not for him to do; he was merely explaining that God loves them and can forgive them for breaking His commands, as He would do any other person. Nevertheless, it would be wonderful if, like others he had come across on the internet, they realised the error they were in and changed as a result.

Going through the statement made by the complainant, Michael remembered on the second occasion they had met, referring to "these two dear men" but denied pointing at them directly. He also recalled the shock and alarm he felt when the two men proudly described in detail their actions with each other, but struggled to understand why if they didn't want their homosexuality to be known publicly they should begin mouth to mouth kissing each other. He also mentioned that the flower-seller was also shocked by the aggression and noise generated by whole episode.

Overall, Michael denied that he had done anything out of order, merely speaking as the Bible commanded, but that this included teaching from Romans 1, that men burning with lust for other men is unnatural. The policewoman then read from the complainant's statement that he was very upset because they were "recently married". Michael instantly responded that they weren't married, because God has deemed that marriage is an institution between man and woman; they therefore only had a civil partnership. The policewoman then went through other statements which emphasised that Michael had said they would burn in hell. He responded by saying that had he really made this statement, the police would have been called a lot quicker than they had been! He denied that he intended to cause alarm or distress to the gay couple, but with hindsight realised that this may have taken place. Nevertheless, he had had conversations with other homosexual men and not had that reaction, with one wanting to talk with him about it on a second occasion. He emphasised that he personally never wants to upset anyone, but is aware that the gospel does sometimes.

Finally, the policewoman asked him whether he realised that mentioning homosexuality on the second occasion he saw the gay couple might get the same reaction that took place during the first very stressful incident in October.

Michael agreed, but stated that he was not accusing the men, merely making an appeal. That concluded the first police interview.

The second interview at Taunton Police Station took place in August 2011. The same policewoman was involved, but this time a duty solicitor was present. Michael was reminded that he had been arrested on suspicion of offences under Section 5 of the Public Order Act, and was duly cautioned. The policewoman explained that the grounds for his arrest were that he had pursued a course of conduct which amounted to harassment by targeting a gay couple, stating that they were sinners and will go to hell and other homophobic comments, and also for making a public spectacle of the same gay couple, causing alarm and distress to the victims. She referred to the statements made by witnesses.

In his defence, Michael said that when they walked directly towards him and were making eye contact with him, he assumed they were coming to talk to him and that is why he spoke to them. Had they been walking, say, 10-15 metres either side of him, he would not have even acknowledged them. By obviously coming to talk to him, he had clearly not singled them out, and he also questioned why they would do so if they felt so strange and embarrassed following the first incident. After all, Taunton has a big, wide High Street and if Michael himself had felt embarrassed by someone, he would have walked on the other side of the street or in the opposite direction. Clearly, instead of embarrassment they were seeking confrontation, and for Michael to say something which they could then turn into the lies and accusations that emerged.

The policewoman then asked him about the flower-seller's reaction to the gay couple's revelations about their private lives. He agreed that he was offended, both by the men's kissing and by "Mike the preacher" not being very nice to the couple, especially as he was using a microphone. The flower-seller also felt that it takes guts to walk down the street holding hands. The policewoman then referred to a witness statement from the same man concerning the second incident on 16th July 2011. As he was bunching up flowers with his colleague, he looked up and again saw the gay couple he remembered from the incident the previous October. He said to his colleague, "Oh no, here we go again", because he knew it would kick off as Mike was preaching. His recollection, though, differed from Mike's concerning whether Mike used the term "homosexual sinners", and indeed he expressed admiration for how calm the men remained. In turn, Mike again denied pointing the finger judgmentally, but explained that referring to the eternal lake of fire is like warning people about to cross a road when a bus is coming – it is vital for their health, and he did so because he cared for people, not to give them nightmares.

The policewoman then referred to a second statement made by an independent witness. She remembered the two males standing about a foot apart, raising their voices, and the preacher saying that it is against God's law for a man to have sex with another man. The witness also recalled the gay couple shouting their annoyance with Michael's judgment of them, and that they had recently been married, but that Michael continued to preach from the Bible. The policewoman wondered whether Michael got so fixated in spouting God's Word that he had no eyes or ears to see or hear what other people were saying. Michael denied that; he could clearly hear what they were saying as they were shouting and screaming abuse at him! He was not judging them but saying that they could be forgiven for their sins. And if he ever saw them again, he would like to give them a hug, say sorry for their being so upset but that their souls depended on believing in God, for Jesus loved them and had received the punishment for their breaking God's commands.

This female witness also recalled a crowd gathering, and that most were more supportive of the gay couple by standing nearer them than him. Michael agreed with this, stating that they were not as aggressive or abusive as the men were, but that two he had met previously – a lad and an older lady – called him names and shouted right in his face. At this point he went quiet, letting them speak for a while before starting to preach again, which led to the crowd dispersing. The lady thought that Mike was homophobic because of what he was saying to the gay couple, but Mike denied this, arguing instead that society has deemed it OK to talk about drunkenness, lies or theft but a preacher may be hated if he talks of sexuality, even though the perpetrators are damaging themselves and going against God.

The witness then went on to state that she has friends and family from different religions and a daughter who is bisexual. Everyone accepts each other for who they are and do not judge. It was not fair to target preaching and upset people. Michael emphasised again that he was not judging but appealing to people, and that the reason people sometimes react in this way is due to guilt, knowing what they are doing is wrong. He recalled two ladies who walk through the town hand in hand, and that he had offered to talk to them about homosexuality. They had declined and walked away, but had not called the police. The men could have done likewise.

Overall, the witness found the incident disturbing and had felt uncomfortable as she doesn't like to see violence or hear shouting and arguing, preferring peace and quiet in the town where she shops. She respected the preacher man for his beliefs, but feels he should respect others' beliefs and sexuality. So the policewoman asked Michael what he thought of other faiths and whether he respected homosexuals. He replied that though he respected other faiths, truth and error exist and the only way to heaven is through Jesus. He has nothing against homosexuals as people, but their actions bring judgment. He agreed with his interrogator that his ultimate concern was that the gay couple don't yet know the man who took their punishment and that they therefore are not going to heaven.

A statement from another policeman was then read out. He had been on foot patrol in Taunton town centre since 2008 and knew of Michael the preacher, mentioning that he had had complaints from businesses concerning the noise linked to his use of a microphone or in shouting at passers-by. At least two people had stopped him over the years after being told that they would burn in hell for breaking God's will, and asked whether freedom of speech extends to preaching about the Bible in an aggressive manner. The policeman had spoken to Michael about the anger and upset he had caused, but he was unrepentant because he was preaching from the Bible.

In response, Michael agreed that his preaching might come across as aggressive because passion and a loud voice in dealing with sensitive subjects may offend some people, but reiterated that he never aimed to be aggressive or upset people and was sad when they did become upset, but he would not compromise what the Bible said. He was also aware that throughout history preaching has offended and that people have been killed and burnt at the stake for preaching the same message as he did today. The gay couple, in his view were not so much upset as in a rage, which was different. And if they were so hurt by what he said the first time, why did they return if it was just to be hurt again? The interview was concluded.

After some time, the case was referred to court, prior to which Michael contacted the Christian Legal Centre for advice. In conjunction with Michael Phillips, a criminal solicitor from Andrew Storch Solicitors, the CLC managed the court process and case on Michael's behalf. Mr Phillips' defence, in January 2012, centred on disputing the exact words Michael was alleged to have used. He also stated that, even if they had been spoken, no offence would have been committed as these views are a statement of orthodox Christian belief, and thus expressing them cannot be an offence. It was also submitted that the prosecution was politically motivated, for Michael's views are contrary to those held by the police and CPS on matters of sexual ethics. This view was supported not only by the fact that no offence had been committed, it was also clear from the way the police reacted – firstly by placating the complainants, to the extent that Michael, the accused, was driven away from the scene, and secondly by commenting that the complainants were happy with this turn of events, whilst making no comment on Michael's response to their actions.

Mr Phillips went on to state that freedom of speech is a fundamental right, and that Michael's free speech rights were violated by police failure to prevent the risk of physical assault and then compounding it by criminal process. Quoting previous cases, he mentioned that citizens are free to express views on morality, and ideas based on Judaeo-Christian morality are protected. Article 9 of the European Convention on Human Rights states that, *"Everyone has the right to freedom of thought, conscience and religion; this right includes freedom to change his religion or belief, and freedom, either alone or in community with others and in public or private, to manifest his religion or belief in worship, teaching, practice and observance."* It goes on to declare, *"Freedom to manifest one's religion or beliefs shall be subject only to such limitations as are prescribed by law and are necessary in a democratic society in the interests of public safety, for the protection of public order, health or morals, or the protection of the rights and freedoms of others*." Essentially, free speech without the right to offend is worthless.

This freedom was put to the test when three women preachers in Wakefield were arrested and then discharged following appearance in the High Court. Without free speech, there would be a "hecklers' veto" and a rush to complain (or even worse) to silence a speaker, which is contrary to democratic society. Adults are free to make personal choices in terms of both faith and sexual ethics.

Judgment took place in February 2012. Michael had not been afraid of the consequences as he had been bought by the precious blood of Jesus. Nevertheless, a great victory for the gospel was given to God's people that day. Michael fails to understand why God should use a nobody, a forgiven sinner like him. Still, God's ways are not our ways.

Since being found innocent in court, Michael has continued to preach Christ's Word with much passion, zeal and fire. God has opened a door, one that he walks through, at times charging. In the face of fierce opposition he refuses to be bowed, and will not let down his Lord who gave his life and blood to make Michael the man he is today. As long as he is led to preach his life-saving message on the streets of this fallen, evil country, he will obey. To God be the glory.

As an addendum, Michael believes the saddest part of this whole episode is the fact that some of his strongest opponents have been professing Christians. He doesn't feel sorry for himself, but is intrigued that unsaved friends and family have shown more outrage at what has happened than supposed believers. He doesn't understand why, but leaves these things to God whilst praying for his opponents. "Come, Lord Jesus, come."

12

Andrew Stephenson
The Pro-Life Activist

Andy was born in Crawley in 1974 but spent most of his early life in Australia before returning to Sussex. His parents were churchgoers, but Andy only discovered faith for himself when it was suggested he try out Jubilee Community Church in Worthing. There he met youngsters simply pouring out their heart to God. Loving Him deeply and determined to know Him better, they attended prayer meetings and read the Bible at home. Seemingly besotted with God, they brought Andy's growing discontent into sharp relief, and as they spoke into his life about sin and holiness, he realised he had a foot in both camps and had a choice to make. When God then showed him a picture of a wide field for him to run into, with Jesus close alongside, his decision was made.

After A-levels, he spent a year as a volunteer doing community work and some evangelism with the church before training as a carpenter and joiner. Working with a small firm making reclaimed pine furniture, he learnt how to fit kitchens and soon had his own business, working with a business partner making bespoke kitchens and other furniture within Angmering Park Estate, an idyllic part of the Sussex countryside.

In 2006, just before he had set up in business, his South African wife Belinda became pregnant with their first child. They had met in a church in Cape Town and married in

1999. For eighteen months they had been trying for a child and were overjoyed as they had almost given up hope. What blew Andy away even more was seeing the unborn baby move on the twelve-week scan. Only then did knowledge of the pregnancy become reality to him. But his excitement would be shattered just a few weeks later when his mother returned from church holding a leaflet showing a twelve-week aborted foetus.

Sick and mystified by this different reaction to pregnancy, he felt compelled to do something. Thinking, naively, that others simply needed to see what he had seen to consider it wrong, he approached his leader at Jubilee, who was very supportive, but then found that the umbrella organisation overseeing Jubilee, whilst strong on church-planting was weak on social action. Nevertheless, he was encouraged and challenged by the words of one church elder: "What do you have faith for?" Essentially, he was asking Andy where he saw this going – and how far did he want to take it?

Andy began to think bigger. Just one leaflet had catapulted him in a new direction. Up to then he had invested his time in work, evangelism and church planting, even discussing with Belinda which country God might be calling them to work in. But as time passed, he sensed that the fight against abortion would occupy him fully, and this conviction was cemented when he listened to an MP3 talk by an American ex-District Attorney, Gregg Cunningham, who had set up CBR – the Centre for Bio-ethical Reform. Gregg's standpoint was simple: until there are as many people saving babies as there are killing them, nothing is going to change.

Gregg's speech kick-started a change in Andy's working schedule. Spending his weekdays as a carpenter, Andy's evenings and weekends became dedicated to Pro-life work. Initially spending time in research and in practising the arguments outlining his position, he and other members of the Pro-life group "Abort 67" first began to demonstrate against abortion in 2007. Beginning in Brighton, the plan was to educate the public concerning the reality of abortion by showing images of aborted foetuses on banners obtained from Sweden. But how would the police and public respond?

Andy needed advice. Gregg knew the UK human rights barrister Paul Diamond, and by 2008 Andy was in contact with the legal team at Christian Concern. Talking about his situation well before his case blew up proved very helpful, with Andrea Williams being able to look at his website and advise on subjects such as the Public Order Act and street activism. It was as if God was giving him advance warning and showing him where to turn in times of trouble. Now for action!

Testing the water, the team decided to cover up the images with pieces of plastic cut to the same shape as the dismembered foetus. Setting up just outside Churchill Square in Brighton, they selected a position alongside a group advertising The Socialist Worker. Thinking them to be comrades, the workers' mood shifted when the banners were unrolled, and they spent the rest of the day encouraging the public no longer to support the postal workers but to support a "woman's right to choose"! Not dismayed by this turn of events, the team were actually grateful, as the added attention it provided led to more people coming to find out what was going on.

On the next occasion, they again set up alongside the Socialist Worker table, but this time exposed the images. When shown what a woman's choice looked like, the mindless chanting ceased; indeed, they didn't say a word. Soon, the group began showing the banners outside abortion clinics. Knowing this would challenge not only abortion supporters but also some Christians, they were encouraged by Proverbs 24:11, which exhorts us to "hold back those staggering towards slaughter." Surely, with children being killed, this was the first place for action. Indeed, Andy emphasises that they do not so much protest against abortion as expose it. And by holding up a picture of an aborted baby, abortion speaks for itself.

As a method, it has proved very effective. Andy recalls taking a call from a woman called Judy Law, who for years has talked to women entering the abortion clinic in Brighton. One day, Judy used some of Abort 67's three inch stickers to show what the British Pregnancy Advisory Service (BPAS) would do to these women's babies should the staff get their hands on them. A young couple on their way to the clinic stopped briefly when she spoke to them and took a sticker of an eight-week aborted foetus. The humanity of the baby and the sheer violence involved persuaded them to call the abortion off. Telling Judy that they had kept the pregnancy a secret, they were now going to tell their parents that they were about to become grandparents. Months later they married, and one Sunday morning a great event took place. During a presentation of Abort 67's work, their precious baby daughter was brought to the front of the church by Judy and shown to the congregation.

Others, too, would respond to what they saw and heard. Andy has lost count of the parents who have changed their minds after being confronted with the truth. Some he would only discover after friends reported their having turned around. The images would also enable people to acknowledge the past. One young man who attended a display in Manchester was very angry and came to talk to them. Doing so changed his mind, and he recognised that abortion killed a defenceless human being. Trembling, he recounted how he had strongly advised a good friend who had got pregnant to have an abortion. She did, and he now felt the pain of responsibility for the death of another. Over the years, the team have come across many people like this university student, who are suffering after being connected with abortion or who are in denial about it. Bringing the issue up helps them realise why they suffer, and often leads to repentance and healing. The pictures can begin to point people back to Christ, again helping to refute the argument that indiscriminate use of the images is counter-productive. Andy feels this is nonsensical, for although the team clearly cannot follow up everyone who views the pictures, God can. And with so many stating that they thought abortion was OK until they saw what it really involved, only a "feelings-led" religion would consider upsetting someone as worse than illuminating people with facts that could save another's life.

The demonstrations became more frequent and Andy knew that his working life would have to change. He tried going half-time, but after only a few weeks knew where his heart lay and he resigned from his carpentry business. By early 2011, he had become a full-time Pro-lifer with Abort 67.

Financially, this was an interesting move! Married, with a family to support, income was required and God provided through presentations and through appealing to donors. At times, survival is precarious, but in faith the organisation has grown to include four volunteers alongside Andy, with hopefully more in time.

The Case

Wistons Clinic is a women's clinic based at 138 Dyke Road, Brighton. Members of Abort 67 had gathered outside the clinic particularly on Wednesday mornings to expose the abortions taking place inside. Standing in two places – at the clinic entrance and on Old Shoreham Road – the group get their point across peacefully to those entering the clinic and passers-by, through conversation, flyers and leaflets, and by showing their banners.

On 27th July 2010, police were called to one of these demonstrations. Police records state that on arrival they found a number of people displaying two banners, each 7 feet by 5 feet in size and containing the logo ABORT67. CO.UK at the bottom. The first banner displayed an eight-week aborted foetus, broken into parts and the size of a coin. The second showed a ten-week aborted foetus, with parts of its body cut away and broken. Both clearly showed limbs, a head, eyes and the torso and intestines, and would clearly have been seen by a large number of pedestrians and passing motorists, as they were located at a busy junction.

While discussing the legalities of the protest with the demonstrators, police were approached by a lady who showed her disgust at the images on display. After receiving other complaints concerning the explicit and distressing nature of the images, police told the protestors to take the banners down and warned them under Section 5 of the Public Order Act. One banner was duly removed but Andy refused to take the second down and was therefore arrested.

A fortnight later, on 10th August 2010, police were again called to the abortion clinic after again receiving complaints about a banner being displayed. After discussion, Andy stressed that it was not their intention to cause alarm or distress but instead to educate and save lives by changing people's minds, should they be arriving for abortion. He agreed to take the banner down but intended to show another in its place. This banner contained an image of an adult palm holding a foetus. Advised that it would most likely cause similar offence, and with other officers arriving at the scene, this banner was removed. Warned that should it be erected, they would be subject to arrest under Section 5, he again unveiled the banner, resulting in his being taken into custody in Brighton.

On 1st June 2011, police were once more called to Wistons Clinic, but on this occasion left the demonstrators alone after having been advised by the Crown Prosecution Service (CPS) that no further action need take place. But the complaints officers received on this day would influence what took place just two weeks later on 15th June. By this point, Andrew had been working with police to reduce public tension. At his own initiative, his group had put up signs warning motorists and pedestrians of distressing abortion pictures ahead, and he had also agreed not to show the images until after 9.30 a.m. (the school run). But he had not agreed to shelve showing the banners completely, and so displayed one as usual. Because of the complaints a fortnight earlier, officers asked him to remove it. He refused and was again reported for offences under Section 5. In addition, the CPS had now authorised a summons on the basis that demonstrators were abusing people's sensibilities, causing harassment, alarm and distress, and so the police seized the sign, along with a camcorder, which his team had been using for evidence.

The next week (22nd June) police assisted once more at the weekly Pro-life demonstration. Two banners were initially being shown – one depicting a seven week embryo in the womb and the other a severed foot of the same age against a coin. But, a little later, the banner showing the aborted foetus in a hand was unfurled. This over-stepped the boundary of what police felt was acceptable and, following a complaint, asked Andy to take it down. Turning the offending image around to face a wall, Andy placed the other banners, along with the public warning signs, in the back of a van, to prevent seizure, before again approaching police and stating that he would be staying for another hour and would display the offending banner for that length of time. Cautioned again, and advised that the banner would be seized under Section 19 as evidence of the offence, Andrew held on to the banner, viewing its seizure as theft. Seen as obstructing the police, both he and his colleague Kathryn Sloane were arrested, handcuffed and placed in the back of a marked vehicle, along with the banner.

A statement from Chief Inspector Simon Nelson sheds light on his dual role in this matter. Police management of protests is strongly influenced by Article 10 (covering freedom of expression) and Article 11 (covering freedom of assembly and association) of the European Convention on Human Rights as set out in the Human Rights Act 1998. Police are also offered guidance by Her Majesty's Inspectorate of Constabulary, which recently stated that, "a procession or assembly should be considered peaceful if its organisers or representatives have peaceful intentions. NB: peaceful includes conduct that might annoy or give offence to persons opposed to the ideas or claims a particular procession is promoting."

Responsible for public order, including the policing of demonstrations, he went on to discuss the protests held by Abort 67 in the Summer of 2010 which provoked extreme public reaction, leading the police to advise protestors that displays went beyond prompting questions and debate, unnecessarily distressing passers-by of all ages to such an extent that it amounted to disorderly conduct. Their refusal to remove the banners led to fixed penalty notices being issued on one occasion and the arrest of two persons on the next.

The Inspector, however, wished to be flexible in his approach. Facilitating discussions between the group and police using a Protest Liaison Officer, he aimed to reduce public tension without suppressing the ability to protest, whilst addressing any unacceptable behaviour of individuals which might constitute criminal conduct. He was clear that on the few occasions when police were not present, the level of public anger towards the group offered an unacceptable risk of a breach of the peace occurring. But he also acknowledged that tensions had been reduced through the group delaying their starting time, restricting images to those showing the foetus in the womb and using warning signs. However, he added that officers had still regularly found themselves having to defend the rights of protestors while members of the public questioned how these are balanced with their own.

In conclusion, he expected the demonstrations to continue and would equally continue to fulfil his duty to those wishing to protest as well as to the wider community.

The Inspector was able to view the argument from both sides. Others chose not to, voicing their disagreement vocally and in written statements to the police. One was a delivery driver who described a banner as repulsive, making him sick to the stomach. His wife had undergone a medically-required abortion some years previously, and the images brought back painful memories. Indeed, only the police presence prevented him from giving in to an overwhelming urge to rip the banner down.

Another felt the demonstrators were wicked. He and his partner had made the gut-wrenching decision to have an abortion and, despite the protests, would do so. One man, whose wife had previously had an abortion, was so upset and agitated that he urged the police to take action, while others stated that the images were aggravating towards the community, upset children and unfairly harassed both clients and staff. One said they were making a terrible day worse, whilst another took issue with Kathryn's tee-shirt bearing the words "Abortion is genocide".

Only one witness was prepared to write anything positive,

appreciating that the demonstrators were saying that it is a child's right to be born. And a police constable in his statement, while personally finding the tactics employed both rude and intrusive, did note that some people seemed happy to talk to the group.

The matter was referred to Brighton Magistrates Court and tried over three days. Andrew faced two allegations under Section 5 of the Public Order Act. Firstly, that on 15th June and 22nd June 2011 he had displayed signs that were threatening, abusive and insulting within sight of a person likely to be caused harassment, alarm or distress. Secondly, for obstructing police on the latter occasion. The District Judge was made aware of the images displayed and of the dialogue with police, whilst also listening to the prosecution's witnesses. Finding there was a case to answer, he turned to the defence.

Andrew stated that he had been involved with Abort 67 for five years. Its aim was to educate about the reality of abortion, using images the public needed to see, as abortion clinics did not give sufficiently detailed information to those considering a termination. Wanting to help women rather than cause them distress, he attended Wistons Clinic twice a week and had also protested outside other clinics and Parliament. Working with police, the changes he had made had helped, whilst their presence reassured him of protection.

He went on to state that graphic images are often shown by newspapers, using the illustration of a war photographer shot dead by a soldier in Burma, and that he was not the first campaigner against injustice, citing the famous examples of Wilberforce (against slavery) and Lord Shaftesbury (against child labour). He had also achieved a measure of success – some women who had viewed the images had decided not to go ahead with an abortion.

Confirming that he had received a fixed penalty notice,

he had not paid the fine, and no prosecution had resulted. Furthermore, when arrested in 2011, he had discussed with police what it was they found so offensive; and that if the pictures do cause such distress, why exactly do we allow abortion to take place? Personally, he too found the images repulsive – the very reason he was trying to change people's minds!

Finally, Andy was aided in his defence by camcorder footage from May 2010, showing a good-natured and calm discussion with a lady and five or six other people reacting similarly on the same day.

In making his decision, the judge referred to a previous case, Brutus v. Cozens, which concerned limitation of freedom of speech and behaviour. The guidance handed down from this case was that speech may be distasteful as long as it is not threatening, abusive or insulting. Remarking that it was up to the prosecution to prove their case beyond reasonable doubt, he stated that whilst the images were graphic and a number of witnesses were upset and distressed, he was not satisfied that the images were threatening, abusive or insulting, as claimed, and thus ruled in Andy's favour. The case was won!

Success in court has proved important to Andy and his team. They are now more confident in dealing with the police, not least in using the imagery, and another unexpected spin-off has been in the reaction of their opponents. Although they disagree with Abort 67's position on abortion, they now see the importance of their case in terms of freedom of speech – the right to communicate uncomfortable issues.

Andy gives all the credit to God for this victory and knows that He will give many more because He is more passionate about children's rights than we are. Truth cannot be held back for long, and Andy fully expects to see legalised abortion confined (in the future) to the pages of history.

But what role should Abort 67 continue to play in God's ultimate victory? Having started in Brighton with few resources and minimal training, the group have connections in many places, including Maidstone, Bristol, Manchester and Wales. More teams are being trained up around the country, and Andy would like to see regular demonstrations outside the Department of Health. Thinking creatively, they were involved in the Paralympics, challenging people that as we celebrate heroes, so we also kill them.

But his primary target has always been the abortion providers. Some years ago, the Royal Mail brought out a stamp celebrating the work of Marie Stopes. Abort 67 responded by doing a photoshoot with the stamp surrounded by body parts. And with Pro-lifers having attended Marie Stopes and BPAS conferences and seen these organisations on the internet stating brazenly that it is alright to kill unborn babies, Andy knows that these powerful organisations can only be stopped in their tracks if public confidence in them is lost. So he aims to damage trust in providers by forcing their leaders to stand up and have to justify publicly what they do.

In his stand, Andy also prays that the church will get involved. So far, sadly, despite his pleas for help, church leaders have failed to engage with him. It may not be a growth strategy for the church, but speaking up for the voiceless remains crucial. However, his relationship with the lawyers at Christian Concern has grown from strength to strength. There for him, and keeping an eye on his legal position, Andy comments that to him they are not merely lawyers who were useful both before and after his arrest, but have become valued partners and friends. He looks forward to the relationship continuing and deepening over the course of time.

PART SIX

INTERFAITH RELATIONS

13

Nohad Halawi
The Airport Beautician

Nohad originates from Lebanon and attended the Lebanon Evangelical School for Girls in Beirut, where assembly involved Bible stories and being taught to treat everyone with respect as children of God. The school allowed her to mix freely with other Christians, Muslims and Druze, all of whom were allowed by their parents to attend assembly like her. When the war began in Lebanon in 1975, she and her sister were sent to board in a convent in Malta, and two years later, in 1977, their parents brought them to the UK where they attended a Christian boarding school for girls.

Nohad has spent all her adult life in the UK and loves having friends from all faiths and races. Having married, she has been strict with her children so that they too respect and tolerate everybody, no matter their religion or culture. As a result, she is known for her love of people and all are welcome to her home.

Along with many other individuals from different cultural and racial backgrounds, Nohad worked within World Duty Free (WDF) and Caroline South Associates (CSA), situated within Terminal 3 of Heathrow Airport. For eight years she loved working at Heathrow. Not only did the airport have a "buzz" about it, but the cosmopolitan atmosphere within Duty Free Heathrow made working there particularly special.

She regarded her colleagues with whom she spent so much of her life as family, but this idyllic working environment did not last. Over a five year period she had noticed a definite change in the mood and ambience around her, following the growth in the airport of fundamentalist Islam. As a result, a climate of intimidation and fear had developed, a situation exacerbated by management treating the faith with privilege and fear. Any criticism of Islam was prevented through severe disciplining, and undoubtedly this single religion was now favoured at Heathrow.

The result of such favouritism has been predictable. Nohad herself had come to the attention of the extremists in April 2010, when she had sought to defend another Lebanese Christian from being bullied, and to prevent the repeated demeaning of her faith. This led to numerous arguments, hostilities and disputes between herself and the fundamentalists over issues like whether being a woman meant implicitly that she should serve a Muslim male. She tried not to be over-sensitive about the daily preaching she received, simply living with it, but nevertheless regarded it as constituting harassment.

One particular individual, however, was particularly troublesome; supporting 9/11 (but blaming the Jews) and upset by the failure of the London bombings in 2005, he represented a clear security danger at Heathrow. Nevertheless, he made the most of his situation and continued with his anti-Christian sentiments, expressing the term "sh*tty Jesus" on many occasions. By December 2010, having suggested that if he hated England so much he should return to Algeria, Nohad and he had effectively ceased speaking to one another. She did talk about her concerns, however, to the Beauty Trading Manager at Duty Free Heathrow. He responded by having what must have been a quiet word with her antagonist in May 2011, but to no effect.

Harassment continued, culminating in an incident taking place five days later.

The Case

On that day, Nohad was having a friendly discussion with a Muslim colleague, whom she described as "Allahwi", a complimentary Arabic term for "Man of God". The conversation took place at her beauty counter and was overheard by another one of the fundamentalists, who mistakenly thought that she had instead said, "Alawi", (which is a Syrian sectarian Islamic group). He immediately interjected with force that she should not be speaking about Islam. Nohad then explained what she had actually said, but despite this explanation being witnessed by a Turkish female Muslim who worked for BA Customer Services, the discussion continued.

At that moment, a manager from WDF passed by and took them into her office to resolve the dispute. Nohad again explained the meaning of "Allahwi", but was amazed when she was accused of saying "sh*tty Islam". With so many Muslim friends, many of them men with whom she would joke over the different fragrances required for their four wives, the idea that she would insult Islam in such a way was laughable. Moreover, she pointed out that the faithful who suffered real abuse and insults at work were Christians, who simply had to live with it. The manager, fortunately, took a professional stand. Accepting that her accuser may have misheard what had been said and over-reacted, she also mentioned that he may have been over-sensitive. The meeting was concluded with both apologising and promising that what had been discussed in the office should remain there.

As far as Nohad was concerned, the matter was closed, but within minutes, her accuser was seen talking with her principal antagonist. Immediately, malicious rumours began to spread. One was that she was anti-Islam. Scared, Nohad now could not look any Muslim in the eye, in case her gesture was misinterpreted. Worse was to come, as her fears were realised: a written complaint to her boss and the WDF Team leader formally accused her of being anti-Islam. While the matter was being investigated, she had her Store Approval Pass removed on a temporary basis.

Statements were taken from the Muslim complainants only. Nohad was not approached, nor required to provide a statement, and instead remained suspended at home until finally asked to provide a statement on 13th July 2011, the day of her hearing. Even then she received very little information concerning the allegations and nothing with respect to the complainants' identities. She suspected bias and that she would not get a fair hearing. The next day her manager permanently removed her Store Approval Pass, without which she could not work, and terminated her employment.

In his letter of 14th July, the trading manager explained the reasons behind this decision. Noting that it was final, he firstly emphasised that names of those involved in the allegations had been removed for their protection; he then alluded to the fateful conversation, noting that it had taken place on a noisy and busy shop floor, and that he understood how a problem over pronunciation could take place. He went on to state that the conversation became heated, a comment Nohad regards as hearsay, and that in the office she had been both unreasonable and offensive in asking her accuser why he was so offended by her using the word "Allahwi" when one of his colleagues regularly employed words in Arabic translating to "sh*tty Jesus". He also took issue with Nohad's use of the word "extremist", in relation to certain people and to her drawing attention to leaflets in her accuser's drawer – a claim that he denied but which had previously been shown to be the case.

Whilst emphasising Nohad's commitment to work and that there was no question over her selling ability, her trading manager was concerned about her conduct on the shop floor. Laying the blame firmly at her door for the breakdown in relationship with some colleagues, and for inappropriate religious conversations that had taken place, he emphasised that all employees should be treated with respect and not offended, even unintentionally.

With her thirteen year unblemished record and character, references seemingly counting for nothing following an unsubstantiated incident, Nohad concluded that she had been unfairly dismissed, discriminated against and harassed. With no chance to defend herself properly, she contacted an Employment Tribunal. Her team mates joined her fight to clear her name by writing letters of support. One anonymous letter concentrated on the failure of her manager to deal with the extremist bullies and mentioned his personal dislike of Nohad. Another letter was far more substantial. Twenty-two colleagues wrote to the General Manager of Terminal 3 Heathrow, making clear their shock and sadness at the recent dismissal of their colleague and friend. They reiterated the unsubstantiated nature of the allegations and that Nohad was not given a fair opportunity to defend herself. Importantly, they went on to state that she had always maintained an excellent relationship with customers, staff and management, treating people with due respect, irrespective of their race, religion or background.

Having underlined her pleasant professionalism, they went further by remarking on WDF benefiting from the wide spectrum of employees, and that they were concerned that any differences in viewpoints should not be allowed to lead to a malicious concoction of lies, aimed at securing the dismissal of a colleague. Use of the "race and religion card" had led to the loss of a valuable member of staff, whose cheerful personality was sorely missed. Since she had left, the work floor was subdued and lacked the harmony and productivity seen previously. In this letter, dated 24th August 2011, her work mates simply urged management to reconsider their decision.

Naturally, the loss was not only felt at work. Nohad was a breadwinner. Struggling financially, she now cannot pay bills and is at risk of losing her home. That alone would be bad enough, but more damage has been done to her personality. Previously effervescent, this happy and positive lady is now much impaired. Stress has brought on depression, anxiety and insomnia, and her sense of vulnerability has led her to be reluctant to trust anyone. Indeed, were it not for the CLC, she reports that she might even have lost her faith in God. Nevertheless, she is at pains to point out that she still loves Muslims, even those who have harmed her, and understands that she must remain civil to them, respecting any differences that they have.

With her airside pass having been removed by an intransigent management, and no apparent way forward for Nohad and her colleagues at work, Nohad sought the help of the Christian Legal Centre. In October 2011, Paul Diamond, acting on her behalf, put her claim for unfair dismissal to an Employment Tribunal, alleging discrimination on a number of grounds relating to race and religion and belief. The hearing took place in April 2012, at which the tribunal heard evidence that Mrs Halawi's working patterns were very tightly controlled by both World Duty Free and Caroline South Associates, indicating she was employed. However, the judge preferred the evidence of WDF and CSA, who argued that she was self-employed and therefore had no protection. That meant that the loss of her airside pass, and consequently her employment, was non-judiciable.

The case was then taken to the Employment Appeal Tribunal, at which Mr Diamond argued that Mrs Halawi was an "employee" or "worker" under European law and as such should be protected from discrimination. Indeed, the whole case depends on her employment rights and the situation remains very complex. At the time of writing, a year later, we are still waiting to hear when the next hearing will take place.

Andrea Williams, Director of the Christian Legal Centre, comments: "Nohad represents tens of thousands of people across the UK who work, in all but name, as 'employees' for companies and yet have absolutely no employment rights. This situation needs to be urgently addressed. But it's also crucial that this case moves on in order for the fundamental security and religious questions it raises to be properly investigated. Heathrow Airport is one of the main points of entry to the UK, so it's vital that any expressions of radical Islamism are investigated and dealt with."

Epilogue

We have seen how thirteen individual Christians in the UK have run into considerable trouble through practising their faith at work or elsewhere in public. Each has gone through a disciplinary or criminal process as a result. Two out of the thirteen – the street preacher and the pro-life activist – have been formally exonerated and still function in the same way as before. For the others, the picture has been very mixed and often pretty bleak.

The city councillor lost the support of her political party but has been able to work as an independent. The teacher lost work but ultimately was given a settlement with the help of the CLC and has been able to earn a living subsequently. One of the two doctors detailed – the community paediatrician – had to retrain as a GP. The magistrate was also able to employ his skills, but only in a reduced sphere. Neither of these two has been allowed to return to the work they loved prior to their cases emerging. The reparative therapist, after several years of trying, has finally been accredited with a new professional body and gained clients again, whilst I continue to practise medicine but with a yellow card attached to my name. Another similar complaint and two yellows make a red.

The other five individuals have been even less fortunate. The nurse, van driver, relationship counsellor and airport beautician all lost their jobs. Two decided to retire rather than fight their battles further, whilst the other two have been psychologically devastated and have struggled to work since. And the foster-parents were not even given the chance to employ the desperately-needed skills that they had previously shown they possessed!

As we reflect on their situations, questions inevitably arise. Why have they been accused either of severe transgressions of rules of employment or some other sort of wrongdoing? What have they actually done wrong? Most, if not all, of the professionals highlighted had excellent work records prior to their crises. Many went far beyond the call of duty in trying to help their fellow man, and not one failed to carry out the job for which they were paid. Sanctioned heavily for their words or actions, is it really the case that anyone truly suffered at their hands? Certainly it could be argued that the teacher's client and my patient were somewhat upset by our ministrations, and that the messages of the pro-life activist and the street preacher deliberately disturbed the ears of the general public. But was it beyond the ken of those who may have been upset to grasp that we were trying to help them? And did not the sanctions received far outweigh any "crime" allegedly committed? Yet each person's stand has been treated as so heinous that at the very least it must never be repeated (my situation) or, more usually, has led to an irrevocable split with some professional colleagues. Why have all thirteen been treated so harshly? To understand the real reason, we must turn to God's Word.

Ever since Adam and Eve, mankind has disobeyed their Creator. In Old Testament times, God sent prophets who spoke out against the utter evil and wickedness perpetrated by rulers. Again and again, these prophets were abominably treated and they needed tremendous courage as they spoke out for God's righteousness, calling their societies to obey Him. Jesus, too, would warn his disciples of the opposition, even persecution, which they were going to face as they faithfully witnessed to his name.

He has been proved right, for since the early centuries of the church, followers of Jesus have often been martyred for their refusal to say that "Caesar is Lord". To affirm instead that "Jesus is Lord" – that he is God, not the state authorities – inevitably has led to the conflict Jesus predicted when he said, "in this world you will have trouble." Furthermore, noting that "no servant is above his master", Jesus knew that what happened to him would subsequently befall his followers.

But while persecution to the point of death is a fact of life for Christians in parts of the world today, martyrdom for believers in the UK is not yet a risk we face. Nevertheless, as we have seen, the right of Christians to go about their daily work acting in accordance with a personal, biblical faith in Jesus Christ is under attack. Christians are being marginalised for their faith with instances in the press almost on a weekly basis. For the cases described here are symptomatic of deep, seismic shifts taking place in our nation.

None of this should surprise Christians, for the Apostle Paul wrote about "principalities and powers" at work behind the scenes. There is a "god of this world" to whom those who oppose God bow in allegiance. But Christians know there is one true and righteous God and it is to Him that they bear witness in their lives and testimony. Strengthened through a real relationship with Jesus, they are enabled to stand against all opposition from ruling elites and from national and supra-national bodies. So they insist on preaching the gospel (the good news), which begins with the bad news that all have sinned and are separated from God the Father, and goes on to declare that only Jesus can save us from our sin, and that this requires us to repent and believe in him. This message is utterly abhorrent to those church leaders who preach a liberal universalism and to secularists, humanists and those preaching other agendas.

Whether the current wave of attacks on Christians in the workplace in Britain will intensify and develop into more life-threatening assaults in these days in which we are living, we cannot tell, but the last book of the Bible provides ample warning of the ultimate outcome. For now, Christians suffer as their hard-won liberties – allowing them to worship, speak of their beliefs and relate to others according to conscience – are not just being eroded but systematically destroyed, with politicians acting as pawns in this process. But at the end of time, when Jesus comes again, the Bible tells us he will only be interested in one thing. In assessing who is fit to enter the Kingdom of Heaven, his criterion is simple. Did you believe in me as Saviour and did you follow me as Lord? For at his name, every knee will bow – and that means every politician, every organisational head, every atheist, every humanist and every secularist who ever fought against Jesus and his followers. All will bow and be ashamed.

I started this book by saying, "It could be you next." With the end in mind, and knowing that Jesus gives abundant life now to his followers, I implore all who read this not to give in to the secular culture in which we live. Be prepared to stand in whatever situation God calls you into. Many more of us will be faced in the future with what I might term "Esther" or "Daniel" situations. Knowing that we represent our Master here on earth, how will you respond? The rest we leave to him.

We hope that you have been touched by the stories in this book. These stories are evidence of a society that has turned its back on God. At Christian Concern we seek to speak of Jesus Christ in our nation's public life as He is the only Hope for our nation. If you would like to find out more about our work and how you can get involved please go to:

www.christianconcern.com

or contact us at

Christian Concern
70 Wimpole Street,
London
W1G 8AX

Tel. 020 3327 1120

5043478R00113

Printed in Great Britain
by Amazon.co.uk, Ltd.,
Marston Gate.